AF480695

# Praise for *Kids Don't Need School*

"I'm already a few chapters in, and it is so hard to put the book down anytime I get started. It's a pleasurable read and the writing style is easy to digest. *Kids Don't Need School* is a wonderful piece of work, and I am certain that anyone who reads it will not only enjoy it but learn something new. Jonathan and Adriana have put in so much thought and dedication into producing this book."

*—Anna G., Cabool, MO*

"This revolutionary book gives you a tour through the current harrowing reality of school and its shocking history and provides you with the valuable skills to use as a parent so that you have a pupil who is willing and able to learn. If you homeschool or are contemplating homeschooling, or if you're a new parent, you will find this book a huge asset.

This is not your average homeschooling book. It gives you the history of school and the present landscape and then hands you the keys to homeschooling your child in a way that makes them a willing pupil. And it explains how you will be able to customize your child's education to serve their needs and those of your entire family. You will feel excited and confident about homeschooling your child!

As a parent, how do you help your child be able to learn just about anything? And how do you get your child to trust you as their mentor and guide in life? This book answers these questions, it thoroughly covers the realm of homeschooling, and shows you how to create a personalized and high-quality education at home for your child. Whether you homeschool already or are contemplating it, you must read this book!

*Kids Don't Need School* will show you the secret to successfully and happily homeschool your child. My family has put this book's advice to the test, and we've been overwhelmed with positive results. It's easier than you think! You just need the wisdom contained in this book. Your child—your family will never be the same."

*—Sysy Muñoz, Roanoke, VA*

"I just finished reading your book and I have to say, I am very impressed with the amount of information and insights you have shared. It's a comprehensive guide for anyone looking to start homeschooling or for those who are already homeschooling and looking for new ideas and strategies—it's basically a homeschool teacher education in one book.

One of the things I appreciated the most is the focus on respecting the child's personal sovereignty and individuality. It's not just about keeping up with public school standards, but helping the child thrive and master the subjects they are interested in. You provide a ton of information on how to motivate children and teach them in a way that they will learn well, considering their individual factors such as stage of development, interests, attention span, and learning style.

I found the book very helpful for my own personal growth as well. Many points on how children learn the best can also be applied when learning new things, myself, and I gained a lot of insights into how to motivate myself when learning new subjects.

The book is also very detailed, yet easy to read and sometimes even witty. You basically answered all the questions that a new or even an experienced homeschooling parent would have, including the worries about socialization and the eternal question of financial aspects.
I would highly recommend this book to anyone who is considering homeschooling or is just interested in learning more about it. It would be very helpful for anyone who is starting or has already started on this journey. Great work, Jonathan, and Adriana!"

*—Rasmus F., Denmark*

"This is the education book I wish my parents had read. I don't say this with any blame. I am certain my parents' educational decisions for me were made with the best of intentions. My family has been homeschooling for nearly a decade, but we didn't start there. I understand well that sometimes we just don't know what we don't know.

This is the education book I wish I had before my first child ever stepped foot into the education system. As someone with years of homeschooling experience, I've found great value in reading *Kids Don't Need School*. I slip into concerns about measuring my children's progress against the standards that were used to measure my own learning. Throughout the book, I found connections that reminded me and reasserted for me why we choose to homeschool and that our top priority is only the best individual interests of each of our children.

Humans are the most successful adaptive generalists on the planet. Our competitive advantage is learning. We are explorers and innovators, overcoming every challenge the universe has thrown at us for as long as we've been anything close to recognizably human. Our ancestors did not need government schools to overcome and integrate the rapid changes they faced, and our children don't need government schools to overcome and integrate the rapid changes they will face.

I often remark that we are seeing childhood be extended into what ought to be adulthood. We create tools and technologies to leverage our adaptability and mastery. But at some point, quite recently, we allowed ourselves to become dependent upon those systems. We no longer transition out of being dependents. I believe the institutional model for education we've been applying plays a significant role in that dependence.

In our dependence on the systems we've created to support us we abandon the things that evolved and emerged, the "what works best for us", to provide the very foundation that made those systems possible. Trading our adaptability for predictability, to better conform to those systems. The well-intentioned damage this does means we end up serving the systems that were meant to serve us. The costs of this abandonment are often not visible for years, sometimes generations. Long enough that it becomes challenging to see the relationship between the cause and the effect.

The Prescott's do a fantastic job of providing the map for how we got here in our approach to education. A map with the detail we require to navigate our way out of the problems of government education and back to healthy models that serve our children instead of serving our systems. The material in this book represents an invaluable educational resource for you as a parent. But far more important than that is the benefit to your child. By implementing what this book offers, your child acquires the most valuable educational tool they will ever have access to, you."


*—Luke Weinhagen, Author of* The Primal Primer

"A practical read that's in touch with todays' challenges; this book is excellent for both newbies and long term homeschoolers who need a refresher and reassurance they're on the right path"

—*Michelle German, Ontario, Canada*

# KIDS DON'T NEED SCHOOL

A Radical New Homeschool Plan to Teach Anything, Promote Independent Learning, and Prepare Children for an Uncertain Future

Jonathan Prescott & Adriana Prescott

Homeschool Life LLC
Kennewick, WA

Homeschool Life LLC
2839 W Kennewick Ave #513
Kennewick, WA 99336
www.homeschoollife.net / www.homeschoollife.us
Send feedback to support@homeschoollife.net

Publisher's Cataloging-in-Publication

Names: Prescott, Jonathan, author. | Prescott, Adriana, author.
Title: Kids don't need school: a radical new homeschool plan to teach anything, promote independent learning, and repare children for an uncertain future / Jonathan & Adriana Prescott.
Description: Kennewick, WA : Homeschool Life LLC, [2023]
Identifiers: ISBN: 979-8-9875906-0-7 (hardcover) | 979-8-9875906-1-4 (softcover) | 979-8-9875906-2-1 (ebook) | 979-8-9875906-3-8 (audiobook)
Subjects: LCSH: Home schooling. | Education--Parent participation. | Parent and child. | Learning. | Educational tests and measurements. | School discipline.

Classification: LCC: LC40 .P74 2023 | DDC: 371.042--dc23

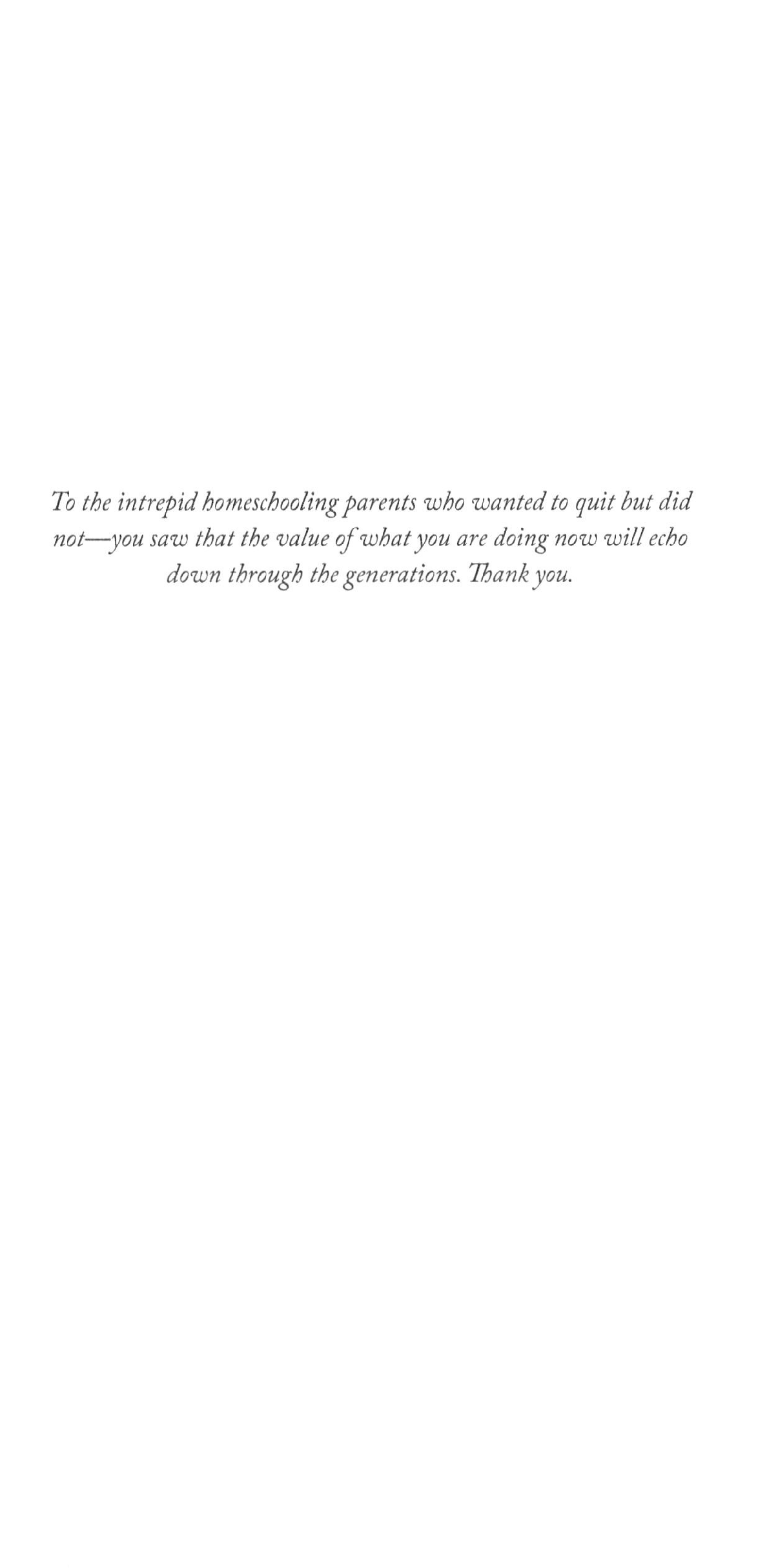

*To the intrepid homeschooling parents who wanted to quit but did not—you saw that the value of what you are doing now will echo down through the generations. Thank you.*

# Tell Us What You Think

Let other readers know what you thought of *Kids Don't Need School*. Please write an honest review for this book on your favorite online bookshop.

# Contents

# Homeschool Beyond the Book

After reading this book, feel free to continue your homeschooling with us.

~Jonathan & Adriana Prescott

- **Homeschooling on a budget?** Subscribe to our FREE email newsletter where you'll get quick, easy homeschool tips and answers to frequently asked questions about raising self-learners. Simply visit **www.homeschoollife.us** to subscribe.

- **Want to connect with 400+ like-minded homeschool parents?** Join the Homeschool Life Community. Your premium membership includes exclusive access to helpful resources, learning courses, useful workshops, and a private forum to ask any question and find the latest homeschooling news, law changes, and trends. Go to **www.homeschoollife.us/become-a-member** to join.

- **Need help now?** The fastest way to get immediate help with and actionable answers to your unique homeschooling challenge is to schedule a private consultation with a husband-and-wife team: Jonathan and Adriana. Book your session at **www.homeschoollife. us/coaching.**

# Elijah Stanfield

The choices a parent makes in the rearing and educating of their own children are so personal and meaningful, I consider them sacred. As opinionated as I am about how my wife and I have chosen to educate our children, I try to be careful not to express those opinions too boldly (if at all) in situations where other parents are explaining the decisions they've already made for their children.

Since you're reading this book, I can assume you're open to considering a radically different perspective on education.

*Kids Don't Need School* is a thorough yet easy-to-read case against compulsory state education and the philosophy and methodology that underpin it—a philosophy and methodology that most parents, even those who homeschool, cannot easily shake.

Why is that?

I liken the emergent "let's recreate the public school classroom but at home" phenomenon to breaking free from a psychological cult or movement. Much of our social, cultural, political, and economic activities and even our relationships revolve around the public school system. When you're in it, it all seems normal—even pleasant, to some. But you'll quickly see how much sway, hold and strength the hivemind social programming is when you try to question, deviate, or completely remove yourself from it, which Jonathan and Adriana Prescott so eloquently advise parents to do.

The sure sign of this education dogmatism is when your choices and beliefs that deviate from the norm are not seen as mere differences of opinion, but are misinterpreted as personal attacks and a threat to the system itself. They're offended, even threatened, simply by you stepping out of their line. They may respond to you defensively—feeling the urge to explain or justify their own choices—criticize you, or accuse you of child neglect and downright abuse. This is in part because they have likely had uncomfortable conversations when their children wondered aloud why they couldn't learn at home. As a result, these parents may have rationalized their decisions by painting homeschooled kids as odd, socially handicapped, economically limited, or even as "special ed."

As a home educator, your very existence is a light that pierces the darkness of the government school institution. Whoever has eyes to see, let him see!

The reality is that we as a civilization are placing our most precious treasures—our children—into prison-like buildings to stand in lines, sit in rows, be monitored, lectured to, and judged. A reality where they will be force-fed propaganda and worldviews that are opposite of your own, will likely be exposed to pornography, and become victims of sexual assault and other manner of violence and abuse. And we willfully send them into that environment six to eight hours a day, virtually everyday, for the entirety of their childhood and beyond. This is communal insanity, and it hurts to admit it.

Youth is a short span of life where we have the most energy, the highest physical capability, a super-boosted mental growth, very little responsibility, and the benefit of a full support team. Yet this is where 90 percent of us were locked away, in a soul-draining jail for kids. What might have we created, accomplished, or become if we were free to develop our own authentic genius? It's only after you break away, step back, and observe with natural eyes that you realize how unnecessary, irrational, and even backward it really is. It was for me.

My school experience went something like this: I sat at my desk almost completely ignoring the teachers for thirteen years. I imagined I was a rock star, a ninja, a superhero. I invented things, created characters, and created stories in my mind. At age six, I started to draw out these thoughts on every surface in front of me, and I never stopped—no matter how many times they punished me or lectured me.

I calculate that I spent at least seven hours a day drawing, resulting in thirteen years of Ds and Fs and every school authority figure telling me that in the "real world," would surely suffer.

In the fourth grade, while everyone else in my class went to P.E., I was sent to the Special Education classroom for "reading help" (It was actually a humiliating psychological war tactic intended to coerce me into paying attention to the teachers and their lessons.).

Fast forward to today: I've been a professional media director, writer, and artist for fifteen years now and in many ways live a charmed life.

Only after many of those years was I finally able to remove from my heart and mind the shrapnel left from the lies told to me, my parents, and the general public about what children must know and become in order to be productive members of society.

I do not regret one single missed homework assignment or failed test. I don't regret faking my way through the reading assignments or copying with my friends' homework to avoid an F. Simply put, I don't regret a single moment I spent being the child I was meant to be. In fact, I'm amazed that I had the resilience to constantly withstand the intense pressure put on me by literally everyone in my life to conform to their educational achievement expectations. I feel sorrow that most children are not able to.

Curriculum. Requirements. Keeping up. Credit. Grades. Reporting. These are concepts of the public school mindset. Implementing this in your home education is the worst of both worlds. You get the limitations and trashy education that the public schools offer while also denying yourself the luxury of a tax-funded babysitter.

There is another way, and that way is simply and clearly outlined here in this book. But I reiterate . . . the rearing of your children is your responsibility, and I cannot know better than you about what is right for your family. Whether you allow your child to attend public school or a private school, or you choose to educate them from home, I encourage you to change your way of thinking and not be swayed by the coercive tactics the system uses. Believe that kids don't need traditional, conveyor-belt style schooling to be educated or socialized. And you don't need to fear for their future without it. Believe that with your support, encouragement, and guidance (and by using the vast resources available on the internet alongside the experiences available in the real world), you can build a trusting relationship with your child based on respect for each other. And that above all else is what will best enable your children to reach their own greatest potential.

This is why I heartily recommend *Kids Don't Need School*. I agree with the message, I enjoyed it, and I know you will, too. It's the essential read for homeschooling families and homeschoolers-to-be.

—**Elijah Stanfield, Illustrator & Co-creator,** *The Tuttle Twins*, **www.tuttletwins.com**

# CHAPTER 1

# Not For Everyone?

"Homeschooling is not for everyone." I have no doubt you've heard this before. Maybe you agree with the sentiment, and taken at face value, it sounds sensible. After all, every family has different needs and values when it comes to educating children. Homeschooling may not be the right choice for every single family.

As founders of the Homeschool Life online community, we get messages like this from aspiring homeschoolers and even veteran homeschool families every single day. We hear it in homeschool groups on social media and in person from local homeschoolers. If you ask what they mean, they'll have some version of these replies:

"It's too expensive. It's a luxury."

"Families with two working parents can't do it."

"It's too hard for most people. You have to readjust your life."

"I don't even think I'm qualified to be a teacher."

"I don't have the space for a setup like that."

When we hear these answers, we sometimes ask, "But what do you mean by *homeschooling*?"

So, what do *you* think when you hear the word *homeschooling*? Do you imagine a school setting, but at home? Maybe you see a large, dedicated space with the conventional look and structure of a traditional school. You have all the subjects, tests, grades, and homework—but at home. Perhaps it's better than a local school environment, at least with a (much) smaller class size. But in your mind, you might imagine the typical K–12 *at home.*

You think about standardized annual tests, followed by attending a homeschool prom, and then summer break. It's recess at a playground outside, timed lunch breaks, and assigned school areas at home. This is what people typically envision. They take the same infrastructure, curriculum and grading . . . and bring it all home. Why?

Is the reasoning for mimicking this kind of school at home based on a fear that a state board of education inspector can check on you at any time? This societal pressure to keep children reading and doing math at their grade level, to keep them from falling behind or redoing grades is intense— even for the stereotypical homeschool family. This mindset creates stress and conflict that is neither fun nor helpful for anyone involved.

This book will argue that none of that is homeschooling. At least, it shouldn't be. We believe that the optimal learning environment for children is *not* a recreation of the traditional school system with the grades, tests, blackboards, field trips, spitballs, a lecturing teacher, and obedient students. All of these things are unnecessary and suboptimal for our children's at-home education. Therefore, most reasons people give for not homeschooling are also illegitimate—they're based on false premises of how we're supposed to teach children and prepare them for life. This book will introduce you to a better way—a very different way—that treats every child as an individual learner with unique needs, abilities, and interests, unlike the typical schoolroom.

And the best part is this different way *works.*

## Meet Alicia

Alicia is a Latina mother of three and a homeschooling parent in the Homeschool Life community. At the time of this writing, she has thirteen-year-old twins (a boy and a girl) and an infant daughter. Her children's homeschool environment looks nothing like the image most people (even current and aspiring homeschoolers) have in mind—because it can't.

Alicia and her daughter both have a lifelong autoimmune disease that, without extremely strict care, becomes life threatening. When it comes to her family's homeschool, nothing looks the way you might expect, beginning with the daily schedule. Alicia and her daughter are unable to sleep through the night because they have to wake up several times to check and manage symptoms. Their diet is also strict. Substituting ingredients because of food restrictions and medications becomes expensive. Alicia's husband has a very demanding job, working long hours to provide for his family. When she can, Alicia supplements the family income through freelance writing.

Alicia and her children's homeschooling experience doesn't resemble "school," but it's not exactly unschooling either. It's clear that, given the severity of their autoimmune conditions, homeschooling is the best option for them to manage their illnesses. Imagine a thirteen-year-old child trying to deal with this in a standard classroom, without the help of her parents. It would be far from ideal, if not impossible. But homeschooling allows Alicia and her children not only to manage their conditions but also to thrive in spite of them. Any child with special needs can not just benefit from home education—in many cases, it's medically necessary for a parent to be with the child to tend to their needs.

So what *does* Alicia's homeschool environment look like?

## Homeschooling in the Real World

Instead of spending hundreds or thousands of dollars on a predesigned curriculum for each subject every year, Alicia's family visits the local library, does online research, has Zoom dates with friends, spends time exploring the outdoors, and does hands-on activities at home. They do this on their own schedule around their own needs.

People often ask, "But what do you do with your children all day?" A better question to ask is, "Why is it strange to be around your children?" Alicia asks even better questions: "What can be said of the typical parent and child relationship out there? Have many lost the ability to spend most waking hours alongside their children? Do they simply lack the confidence or vision of how to do so? Have we been overly reliant on material forms of motivation?"

Instead of lecturing her twins, having them complete assigned work, and then be tested, it's family time all the time. Books are open; Mom and Dad are reading and learning right along with the children, researching online about their chicken coop and caring for their chickens. They even have remote friend groups they join online where everyone bakes a cake or plays Minecraft together. In this homeschooling environment, learning is fun, collaborative, and cooperative. And it's not isolating, like some might think.

Instead of trying to schedule complete lesson plans with one subject having an allotted time before moving on to the next, Alicia and her children get to be flexible. She's able to observe what her children are interested in. They study according to their attention span for any given subject on any given day, and there's no required sitting down at a desk or table quietly. Any kid would agree that's boring.

With this way of homeschooling, learning becomes . . . fun. Alicia's children learn more and have more fun because they want to learn. It's better than what a certified teacher can do—they're not trained to help children become self-motivated learners who pursue mastery because they want to. And that's exactly what Alicia has been able to do.

Alicia's story shows that anyone can make homeschooling work because homeschooling can be so different from what most parents believe it should be. This misbelief that homeschool is schoolwork at home comes from a misunderstanding of school itself. We want you to break out of this social conditioning of what society says school is and realize why your kids don't need it.

# Why Children Don't Need School

Many of you already know why you don't want your children in the public school system or why you don't want them to go back. It probably includes some of the following facts, yet some of these may be new to you, shocking, or even encourage a renewed commitment to homeschooling. The bottom line is that schools fail in many ways, despite the billions of dollars we throw at them. The audacity is that they claim that any shortcomings on their part are actually your fault for not funding them enough. Let's pull back this curtain:

- The US, where the majority of children attend public (69.4 percent) and private (10 percent) schools, ranks near the bottom in math, science, and reading in comparison to other industrialized countries. The US has ranked low in these areas since 1967.[1,2,3,4,5]

- Common Core uses test scores as a subpar way to measure aptitude. (In reality, Common Core is a cash cow for its creators, in part because schools purchase Common Core curriculum from them.[6,7] The fall of American students' scholastic achievement has coincided with the rise of the education NGO—it took only fifty years to create the education-industrial complex).[8]

- Only 13 percent of American high school students are proficient in US history.[9] Those who forget the cycles of history are doomed to repeat them, and the public education system seems to be working hard to achieve that.


1   "Number of Public Schools in the US: Key 2023 Data on States & Demographics," Research.com, September 26, 2022, https://research.com/universities-colleges/number-of-public-schools-in-the-us#:~:text=Public%20Primary%20School%20Statistics,-Public%20primary%20schools&text=As%20of%20late%2C%20there%20are,enrolled%20in%20public%20primary%20schools.
2   "Digest of Education Statistics," National Center for Education Statistics, n.d., https://nces.ed.gov/programs/digest/d16/tables/dt16_205.10.asp?current=yes.
3   Jill Barshay, "US Now Ranks Near the Bottom among 35 Industrialized Nations in Math," The Hechinger Report, December 6, 2016, https://hechingerreport.org/u-s-now-ranks-near-bottom-among-35-industrialized-nations-math/.
4   Moriah Balingit and Andrew Van Dam, "US Students Continue to Lag behind Peers in East Asia and Europe in Reading, Math and Science, Exams Show, Washington Post, December 3, 2019, https://www.washingtonpost.com/local/education/us-students-continue-to-lag-behind-peers-in-east-asia-and-europe-in-reading-math-and-science-exams-show/2019/12/02/e9e3b37c-153d-11ea-9110-3b34ce1d92b1_story.html.
5   Jill Barshay, "What 2018 PISA International Rankings Tell Us about US Schools," December 16, 2019, The Hechinger Report, https://hechingerreport.org/what-2018-pisa-international-rankings-tell-us-about-u-s-schools/.
6   Utahns against Common Core, May 10, 2018, https://www.utahnsagainstcommoncore.com/california-a-case-study-in-how-common-core-decimates-math-progress/ca-calculus/.
7   Lawrence Delevingne, "Companies Cash In on Common Core Despite Controversy," CNBC, last updated March 12, 2015, https://www.cnbc.com/2015/03/11/companies-cash-in-on-common-core-despite-controversy.html.
8   Rick Hess, "How the Failure of the Common Core Looked from the Ground," Education Week, May 19, 2021, https://www.edweek.org/teaching-learning/opinion-how-the-failure-of-the-common-core-looked-from-the-ground/2021/05.
9   Christine Armario, "Report: Students Don't Know Much About US History," NBC News, June 14, 2011, https://www.nbcnews.com/id/wbna43397386.

- Public-schooled children fall far behind homeschooled students in communication ability, daily living independence, life maturity, and—surprisingly, to some—socialization.[10]
- What is perhaps the greatest failure of school in this country is this: 54 percent of American adults can't even read.[11] At the time of this writing, more than 130 million adults "lack proficiency in literacy," meaning they cannot read and comprehend anything higher than sixth-grade material
- Meanwhile, the US outspends most other countries on education, even countries that rank higher.[12] Public schools spend $13,701 per student, yet homeschool families who spend less than $600 per year per student see their students reach the 86th percentile on test scores. Their peers in the public school average in the 50th percentile on test scores.[13,14,15]
- Property taxes have risen out of control in every state in an effort to put more money into schools, and yet education isn't improving. Despite almost unlimited, per-student funding, improvements in education are not actualized.[16]

The bottom line is that public school "excellence" is a scam—and you are paying a lot for it.

After rising every year for fifty years, US student scores on a variety of achievement tests dropped sharply in 1967.[17] This included the first international comparison of educational achievement in math, in which the

10  Wes Mayberry, "Number of Homeschooled Children in US Continues to Grow," Jackson County Sentinel, July 24, 2015, http://jcsentinel.com/feature_story/article_d2463792-3204-11e5-ad03-6ffafbeb6431.html.

11  Michael T. Nietzel, "Low Literacy Levels among US Adults Could Be Costing the Economy $2.2 Trillion a Year, Forbes, September 9, 2020, https://www.forbes.com/sites/michaeltnietzel/2020/09/09/low-literacy-levels-among-us-adults-could-be-costing-the-economy-22-trillion-a-year/?sh=58e429a04c90.

12  Linda Gorman, "Education," Econlib, n.d., https://www.econlib.org/library/Enc/Education.html.

13  National Center for Education Statistics, "Public School Expenditures," US Department of Education, Institute of Education Sciences. Last updated May 2022, https://nces.ed.gov/programs/coe/indicator/cmb..

14  Brian D. Ray, "Research Facts on Homeschooling," National Home Education Research Institute, September 15, 2022, https://www.nheri.org/research-facts-on-homeschooling/#:~:text=Taxpayers%20spend%20nothing%20on%20the,resources%20for%20their%20children's%20education.

15  "Some Fascinating Facts about Homeschool vs Public School," Homeschool World, n.d., https://www.home-school.com/news/homeschool-vs-public-school.php.

16  Michele Lerner, "Property Taxes on US Homes Rose to $328 Billion in 2021, Report Finds," Washington Post, May 5, 2022, https://www.washingtonpost.com/business/2022/05/05/property-taxes-us-homes-rose-328-billion-2021-report-finds/.

17  Gorman, "Education."

United States ranked eleventh out of twelve nations—nearly the lowest.[18] Students in Germany, England, France, and Japan all scored ahead of students in the US in math. The only country behind the US was Sweden. A Washington Post news article explained that US teachers weren't as well trained in math pedagogy and that American society didn't value mathematical achievement as much as other countries.[19]

> "What surprises me is how stable US performance is," said Tom Loveless, an education expert who was formerly at the Brookings Institution. "The scores have always been mediocre."[20]

In the 1980s, economists, puzzled by a decline in the growth of US productivity, realized that American schools had taken a dramatic turn for the worse. They noted the decline in achievement tests that began in 1967.[21] They continued to decline through 1980. The decline was so severe that students graduating in 1980 had learned "about 1.25 grade-level equivalents less than those who graduated in 1967." Although achievement levels began to recover in 1980, the recovery has been weak, and student achievement has yet to regain 1967 levels. By the turn of the century, conservative estimates of the economic growth loss as a result of the academic achievement decline were on the order of 3.6 percent of the 2000 gross national product.[22]

> The characteristics of the educational productivity decline challenged widely accepted educational theories of school performance. Theorists who were accustomed to blaming increased poverty, family instability, large class size, and insufficient spending for poor school performance could not explain why the scores of more able students declined at least as much as those of less able ones or why measures of inferential ability and problem-solving declined more than those of simpler tasks.

The United States spends more and more on education per student, but our return on investment is dismal by every measure you can imagine. The

---


18  Barshay, "What 2018 PISA International Rankings Tell Us."
19  Valerie Strauss, "Why the Common Core Standards Failed—And What It Means for School Reform," Washington Post, April 5, 2021, https://www.washingtonpost.com/education/2021/04/05/common-core-failed-school-reform/.
20  Barshay, "What 2018 PISA International Rankings Tell Us."
21  Gorman, "Education."
22  Ibid.

argument in favor of school is that it prepares students to hold down a job in the real world. But how many professions do you know that require work to be taken home and done outside working hours?

As statistics from just that thirteen-year period of 1967 through 1980 show, school does not, in fact, prepare children for the real world. And it's only gotten worse since the dawn of the information age, worldwide internet connectivity, and social media. Teaching quality falls behind; the country's children fall further behind.

If children in the United States don't receive a complete education for the real world at school, what do they get instead?

What could be the benefit to children in being away from their parents and their home for long periods of time, every day, every year? Children are being conditioned early in life to be away from their homes and to be influenced by those watching them. When they come home from school at the end of the day, they often experience or have experienced the following:

- Emotional and social struggles from being away from the comfort of home and family
- Struggle with motivation to complete homework
- Struggle with learning new material
- A dislike of learning
- Physical and mental exhaustion from completing the demands of school
- A lack of excitement toward the monotony of their schedule
- Constipation and bladder infections because of restricted bathroom access
- A desire for more time spent with parents to talk about each other's day and have meaningful conversations
- Conflicts from parents not being understanding of and empathetic to their needs
- Feelings of stress and anxiety from not being able to meet demands and expectations
- Distress from peer conflicts, bullying, loneliness, isolation, and ostracization

- Conflicts with poor-quality, underperforming teachers
- Weight and health issues due to poor nutrition choices offered
- Not having their special needs, or other specific needs met

These schools are babysitting services. They not only lack the capacity to educate children, but the public school system is also not cheap. This is despite what the term "free public education" leads some to believe.

Property taxes are a considerable annual expense for homeowners and even renters, albeit indirectly. We don't get anything close to what we're paying for. What we've ended up getting is a nation of children who have never been inspired or motivated to study beyond what is "going to be on the test." This is a complete tragedy.

In contrast, every parent knows that children have no problem picking up and reading books if they love to read. If children are read to by their parents early on and often, they learn to love reading. Children can then learn a lot of things independently just by reading a variety of books. This is one way parents have the ability to influence their children in a positive way and promote independent learning. The love of learning and exploring new things happens naturally—if it's not conditioned out of them. School destroys this love of learning through rigid curricula and mountains of homework assignments.

The bottom line is that children need their parents to care for them to nurture the bonds of family and the love of learning. These are the requirements that children need satisfied so they don't suffer negative outcomes from attending school.

There is another adverse reaction that few like to talk about when children attend a traditional school—a low and continuing degradation of social trust. Renowned journalist, author, and culture critic Michael Malice published the following observation on Twitter:

> Public schools are literal prisons for children and the only time many people will ever encounter physical violence in their lives.[23]

---

23 "Public schools are literal prisons for children and the only time many people will ever encounter physical violence in their lives." (@michaelmalice, July 5, 2019).

The social structure in federal prison is paralleled in school cliques. Just like in prison, children separate themselves into groups based on a variety of factors—race, looks, socioeconomic status, abilities, clothing—you name it. We see this reflected in pop culture in movies like *The Breakfast Club*, *Mean Girls*, and pretty much any other movie involving school-aged children. The obsession with identity creates division and fosters a bullying environment. This is convenient for those in charge because it creates a divide-and-conquer mentality that follows them into adulthood. If people are too busy fighting over stupidities like skin color and brand names, what kind of well-adjusted, functioning society do we have? When these things become focal points in children's lives, they take precedence over the things that really matter and distract them from learning and growing as individuals.

The school that children don't need includes the one that most homeschool families are convinced they *do* need. We mean that literally—school as we know it is *not* something children need. So if it's so unnecessary and so destructive to our children and to our society at large, why is school like this? How did it become the way that it is?

# The Dark Origins of Modern Schooling

The school system of today descends from a framework most parents have never heard of—the Prussian model of education. It's been around for so long, some are noticing that it's worn out its welcome.

So what is this model, and what's the problem with it?

The Prussian model of education came about in the eighteenth century, in the German kingdom of Prussia, after the bloody Napoleonic wars which brought about the coming of a new world order. The Prussian model's founding principles were laid out by eighteenth-century philosopher Johann Gottlieb Fichte. Its main characteristic is that it was developed as *mandatory* education: every individual among the lower classes was required to attend school up to a certain level. The Prussian school system was funded through taxes, so citizens could attend for free. It included at least eight years of schooling that were supposed to prepare students for the modern world.

Apart from teaching key subjects like mathematics, reading, and writing, it also taught ethics, obedience, and duty to your country. This is where many take issue with the system. Ira David Socol, educational author, blogger, and learning environment specialist wrote recently in his Essay in Medium, "The Prussian Model and the Failure of Personal Ethics," Socol argues that this model wasn't really about education but compliance.

Born of Prussia's military failings in the Napoleonic wars, the German kingdom developed an "education" system designed to indoctrinate children, year by year, from age six to sixteen, into full compliance with the state and its military leaders. The point was, bluntly, to ensure that "no German soldier would ever disobey an order again."[24]

Socol even claims this model is what allowed World War II to take place—doing your duty for the country came at the expense of doing what was right. And we all know the horrors that happened because of that emphasis on duty. The system created not only obedient conformists but also an environment in which independent thought was crushed, and students felt the social and authoritarian pressure to obey orders.

The great Bertrand Russell succinctly summarizes Fichte saying:

> Fichte laid it down that education  should aim at destroying free will so that after pupils are thus schooled they will be incapable throughout the rest of their lives of thinking or acting otherwise than as their school masters would have wished.[25]

He also wrote:

> Real education must start by getting to the source of human nature. Education must exert "an influence penetrating to the roots of vital impulse and action." Here was a great failing of traditional education, for it had relied upon and appealed to the student's free will. "I should reply that that very recognition of, and reliance upon, free will in the pupil is the first mistake of the old system. Compulsion, not freedom, is best for students.[26]

---

24  Ira David Socol, "The Prussian Model and the Failure of Personal Ethics," Medium, August 5, 2018.
25  Russell, Bertrand. Essay. In The Impact of Science on Society, 1st ed., 50–50. New York, NY: Routledge, 2016.
26  Hicks, Stephen R.C. Explaining Postmodernism: Skepticism and Socialism from Rousseau to Foucault (Expanded Edition). Ockham's Razor Publishing, 2010.

He continued:

> Unfortunately, it is difficult to do this under contemporary living arrangements, in which children go to school and then return to corrupting influences in their homes and their neighborhoods at the end of the day.[27]

"It is essential," Fichte then urged, "that from the very beginning the pupil should be continuously and completely under the influence of this education, and should be separated altogether from the community, and kept from all contact with it."[28]

This Prussian model of education eventually became the education system in most modern nations, including the United States. In the United States, the Prussian model was imported and adopted by Horace Mann, known as the father of public education. Mann's core concept was that "the State is the father of children" and that it is the responsibility of the state to ensure that education is provided to the child. It was Mann who was influential in making school attendance legally mandatory, common, and paid for by public dollars.

After Mann's common school movement, progressivist John Dewey finished up the foundations for the modern school model. Dewey is known for advocating for public schools to be a vehicle for social change, noting:

> Education is a regulation of the process of coming to share in the social consciousness; and that the adjustment of individual activity on the basis of this social consciousness is the only sure method of social reconstruction.[29]

As a result of Fichte, Mann, and Dewey, we birthed a controlling Prussian system, made compulsory by the state, funded by our taxes, with a mission for societal change.

This same Fichte-Mann-Dewey beast still exists in our schools today. Because it continues to indoctrinate rather than to truly educate children, it simply doesn't work. The failings of this system have become so apparent

---

27  Ibid.
28  Ibid.
29  John Dewey, "My Pedagogic Creed," School Journal 54 (January 1897): 77–80.

that homeschooling has exploded exponentially in the US in recent years. Yet this model has been so dominant in our lives, parents often struggle to step away from that structure, even if they understand the need to create a unique learning environment. Trying to recreate this environment when you homeschool your children defeats the purpose of homeschooling in the first place.

So much of the Prussian model is about elite versus commoner; there's a deep classist nature to the system. The working class were trained to be tools of the state and to be used to the government's ends, benefitting the elite and no one else. It's the ultimate form of exploitation because it operates under the guise of education. What it really does is educate the masses into submission. Meanwhile, wealthy aristocrats excused their children from public education and hired private tutors instead. They wanted their children to enjoy a leisurely, carefree childhood, free from a schoolhouse instructor's switch while also pursuing what came naturally to each child.

So no, the Prussian model is not about education or preparing children for the real world. It is at best a mediocre babysitter and at worst a soul-crushing prison system designed to make obedient factory slaves out of our children—ones who will not question the orders given to them. It has disguised itself as a net positive for society and something necessary. But after decades of underperforming schools, continuing literacy issues, postgrad disappointments, the explosion of bullying, and dismal, dropping test scores, it's safe to say parents—and students themselves—are starting to see how this system is a failure at the task for which it was sold to us, the taxpayers: as the best preparation for our children's future. This is all at the cost of the chains of taxation on our very homes into perpetuity—a lien on our largest physical investment—year after year, forever.

There remain many unanswered questions and other things we are just so used to that we take them as normal of our government-run education monopoly, such as; Would the vocal political proponents of the public school system ever send their children to public school? If they believe in the system so much, why wouldn't they send their children there? No, they know it's a garbage system, and keeping their own children away from it is admitting so. Nevertheless, there are many aspects of traditional school that we regular folk don't question, yet when we look closely and analyze each part, they don't make sense. At the very least, we can clearly identify, analyze, and question the different approaches that we can take beyond the standard accepted protocol.

For an example of this analysis, why do schools start early in the morning and end in the afternoon? Is that optimal? Does it have to be a continuous day, or can it be split up differently? Why do we take summers off? In homeschooling, summer can be the best time to take the learning outside and explore the outdoors. Beautiful, sunny weather is the best time to combine quality education with quality family time.

Proponents of traditional schools emphasize the mantra, "School sports breed character!" While it's true that children need exercise, play, fitness, and social interaction, having a multimillion-dollar high school football program is not serving education—even the most ardent public school supporters criticize the emphasis on sports over academics. I agree. It's a distraction. Children don't learn proper fitness and nutrition habits from trying to be the star quarterback, and it's quite common to pick up some negative character traits such as the contribution to cliques and the classic jocks-versus-dorks scenario.

"But what about the arts?" While it is true that sports, music, and creativity are enriching hobbies, they are not always something to be relied on in the real world. As important as they can be, sports and creative arts programs do not prepare children for life on the whole. Only a small fraction of athletes and artists ever make a living in (what has evolved to be) the professional mass media "bread and circuses"—entertainment intended to distract the masses from civilization collapsing around them. The phrase was first used in the fall of ancient Rome but applies equally to Western culture today. It's rough out there, and we need a different way to think about how we promote, emphasize, and highlight what is valuable and virtuous, rather than the distractions that are being used against us.

In the context of this book, the recent major world events that our students have had to survive are a global pandemic, supply chain collapse, inflation, food shortages, impending famines, collapsing economies, and a real threat of World War III. Yet every day, the media parades in our faces more and more sports, celebrities, and other distractions. When not fearmongering the public on various issues, they aim to distract us with dumbed-down, drama-filled entertainment. Typical schooling doesn't teach children to see through the fog of fame. Peer pressure, together with overemphasis on hobbies in school, funnels children into that fog—if anything, their schooling teaches them to put their heads down and just do the assignments as they were told to do.

There's also the manufactured distraction of modern art. What passes for art today—a banana peel duct-taped to a white wall, a hodgepodge of big red structural beams? This "anti-art" is a social engineering tool to disrupt any connection a person has to their cultural past and heritage—a Marxist idea that permeates higher-education curricula—whereas a classical education that explores quality art, architecture, and design throughout centuries and different time periods has been lost to postmodernism in the humanities. The same goes for sports and gym class. What kind of sports are children playing, and are they effective as exercise? Could students benefit from a more individualized fitness plan that involves weightlifting, or how about a sport or activity they truly enjoy?

> "Well, I'm not some 1950s-model homemaker," you might be saying. Who said homeschooling requires a mother to cosplay as the perfect 1950s homemaker: the father going off to his nine-to-five career, and the perfectly coiffed wife cooking, cleaning, and taking care of the household? That's not what we advocate for. In fact, throw away the homemaker image altogether. In the 1950s, the wife was home alone all day, and the children were in school. No, real home-based education is as flexible and customizable as you want it.

What really matters for homeschooling families is household harmony, not through authoritarian edicts but through strong parent-child relationships. What we've discovered missing from traditional schooling is the proper transition from an enriched childhood to a self-sufficient adulthood. In more recent years, there's been a marked increase in complaints from people about how the school system failed them. Many have asked why schools don't put more emphasis on financial literacy, like retirement and investing. Many have realized that school wasn't about preparing them for the real world. Many lack critical thinking skills.

There's simply no variation or flexibility in the Prussian model that offers children and their families an education in how to be a self-sufficient adult and thrive in the world, no matter the circumstances.

Children don't need school. So what do they need instead?

# CHAPTER 2

# What Children Need Instead

If children don't need school, then what do they need? This is the natural question to ask yourself at this point—and the central question of this book. The answer hides in plain sight. What children need instead of the oppressive, creativity-killing, Prussian schooling is for parents to believe that they themselves are capable of providing a high-quality education tailored to their children—one that will prepare them for whatever future may come.

But once parents realize their children are better off receiving a home education, self-doubt sets in. "But I'm not a qualified teacher" is often the otherwise-eager-to-homeschool parent's number one objection to it. Yet it's clear that their children do not need public school.

The COVID-19 pandemic and school closings were eye opening for millions of parents. We witnessed our children start to recover from their school-induced mental trauma. That's no exaggeration. The effects of this unprecedented event were striking enough to break a parent's conditioning. We started asking questions like, "Why are my children walking around like they have PTSD?"

Parents started to notice that the schools had a strange hold on their children. They began to notice the once-close relationship they remembered having with their children prior to their attending school was different—and the parent had been so busy with other work, they didn't notice the loss of connection. Now that they were all home, it became obvious. Parents realized that the family, once the foundation of society, had been undermined and usurped by government school. Over the past several generations, we went from strong parent-child bonds to broken and dysfunctional homes. Instead of being honored, the family was mocked and denigrated as something to be avoided. Having children and starting a family was being touted as "oppressive to women" or "bad for the environment."

Regardless of how the social engineers were framing it, the fact remained: the school system continues to rob families of 16,000 hours together. That's the approximate number of away-from-home hours for K–12 students (not including homework time). Parents began to see during the lockdowns that they no longer knew their own children—they started to see the results of the 16,000 hours. The children were now peer bonded and teacher bonded, but more than that, parents saw that their own children viewed them with contempt and disdain. This disconnect, once thought to be just part of growing up, was now viewed in its true light—a glaring relationship hole. Parents ask, "What happened? Why does it seem that my relationship to my children and later to my teenager is strained and growing distant?" The simple answer is that we have been outsourcing our parenting role to government schools all this time.

As we learned in Chapter 1, Horace Mann installed Fichte's Prussian model of compulsory, institutionalized education. This Mann-Fichte system propagandizes children to replace their natural agency with conditioned compliance and was designed to replace commitment to family with duty to the state.

Parents and children don't realize the cognitive dissonance this system forces on the developing mind until they're released from its grasp. It usurps the family as the foundation of civilization and undermines parental authority. The state replaces the parents and destroys their bond with the child. No other education system in the history of mankind was designed for such a purpose.

Now is the time to take action, undo the damage, and restore our relationships with our children. Each family's stability affects society and contributes to the health of the whole. The founding fathers and the Greeks knew this too. We must return to a strong, wise set of common values. It starts when we make loving parent-child relationships paramount again. Connecting or reconnecting to your child is parenting. And it's the answer to the opening question. Your children don't need the school; they need their parents. They need *you*.

# Homeschooling Is Parenting

Or we could say that *education* is parenting. We know this with infants and toddlers—for example, was it a chore for your child to learn how to walk? Were there potty training tests? Did you need a workbook to learn how to use a fork? Flashcards for combing hair? But I digress.

What your children need as they develop into older children, teenagers, and adults is what you've already been giving them. So how do you continue teaching your children as they grow? The answer is not the way you'd expect.

When you reestablish the parent-child bond, you become someone your children want to learn from. Be the model for the behavior you value, and they'll be inspired to keep learning, even on their own in subjects they haven't yet mastered. Children need their parents, period. You should be their template for adulthood, not some stranger in an institution that doesn't have their best interests at heart.

Children want to be in the safety and comfort of their homes. They want to be around the people they trust, love, and care about. It's in that kind of environment that the bonds between parents and children can be strengthened.

The thousands of hours most children spend in school place a wedge between them and their parents. The children form bonds with their peers instead, which can lead to friction in the parent-child relationship.

Peers may not be the best influences. You can be sure they don't bring the wisdom and life experiences you can provide.

Only parents can teach their children the lessons they need to have the best life outcomes. Therefore, the family is the best place to learn skills, knowledge, and traditions. That's how legacies and pride in family accomplishments are passed on.

## What about Discipline?

We believe that healthy parent-child relationships need to be free of violence, coercion, yelling, hitting, and/or spanking. It is necessary to cease the violence toward each other—healthy relationships do not require hitting. This is commonly called peaceful parenting.

A healthy parent-child relationship lowers stress and promotes creativity. To have this type of relationship, parents must use peaceful parenting. No aggression—violence, spanking, corporal punishment, yelling, time-outs, ultimatums, ridicule, coercion—should be used because it negatively affects children's development.

What if you've practiced nonpeaceful parenting? Perhaps you're worried that anything resembling gentle parenting will make your child dependent, entitled, or needy. And if you don't discipline your children, how will they learn how the real world works?

Here are two of the best research-based cases against spanking:

The first case explains that spanking causes behavioral problems and that parents who spank their children think they need to impose harsher and harsher punishments to fix the behavior that spanking caused in the first place. The following excerpt from a study on spanking illustrates its detrimental effects on children.

> In a comprehensive meta-analysis of 50 years of research summarizing the corporal punishment literature, including both US-based and international studies conducted with 160,927 unique children . . . spanking was consistently associated with negative outcomes for children, including more internalizing and externalizing child behavior problems, antisocial behavior, and child aggression. Studies of US samples revealed that having a history of being spanked as a child is associated with mental health problems and antisocial behavior in adulthood. . . . Even low levels of spanking were associated with higher externalizing

> behavior. . . . Overall, the literature demonstrates that spanking is harmful for children, but, again, this knowledge is primarily based in the context of high-income countries.[30]

Spanking is so detrimental to childhood development, it's now officially considered an adverse childhood experience, alongside parental drug abuse, neglect, and hunger.[31]

The second case is that spanking lowers IQ.[32] The IQs of younger children who were spanked were 5 points lower on average four years later than those of children of the same age who were not spanked. Scores among older children were an average of 2.8 points lower among spanked children than children who were not spanked.[33]

Parents are spanking their children *out of* the capacity for independence, critical thinking, and self-discipline. They are potentially driving children into lives of crime that rob them of opportunities.

But some violence-prone parents who believe corporal punishment isn't that bad might say, "But I was spanked and turned out OK." Well, that anecdotal response might actually be cognitive dissonance talking. Even if your mom hugged you after she spanked you, she still used aggression. Maybe your dad said, "It's for your own good." Gaslighters say the same to their victims. Keep in mind that abuse and trauma are dose dependent—the more trauma, the more it shows.

People imitate the same behavior they were subjected to. You were spanked; now you're spanking your children. To consider an alternative— that you were wronged, and you are wronging your child—is too much to handle.

Plus, people don't realize how many failed relationships they've had or how they've learned to lie and manipulate to feel safe in adult relationships.

---

30  Garrett T. Pace, Shawna J. Lee, and Andrew Grogan-Kaylor, "Spanking and Young Children's Socioemotional Development in Low- and Middle-Income Countries, Child Abuse & Neglect 88 (2019): 84–95. https://doi.org/10.1016/j.chiabu.2018.11.003.

31  Tracie O. Afifi, Derek. Ford, Elizabeth T. Gershoff, Melissa Merrick, Andrew Grogan-Kaylor, Katie A. Ports, Harriet L. MacMillan, George W. Holden, Catherine A. Taylor, Shawna J. Lee, and Robbyn Peters Bennett, "Spanking and Adult Mental Health Impairment: The Case for the Designation of Spanking as an Adverse Childhood Experience, Child Abuse & Neglect 71 (2017): 24–31, https://doi.org/10.1016/j.chiabu.2017.01.014.

32  Elizabeth T. Gershoff and Andrew Grogan-Kaylor, "Spanking and Child Outcomes: Old Controversies and New Meta-Analyses," Journal of Family Psychology 30, no. 4 (2016): 453–469, https://doi.org/10.1037/fam0000191.

33  "Children Who Are Spanked Have Lower IQs, New Research Finds," paper presented at the Fourteenth International Conference on Violence, Abuse and Trauma, San Diego, CA, September 25, 2009, https://www.sciencedaily.com/releases/2009/09/090924231749.htm.

Spanking doesn't teach you those things are wrong; it teaches you to avoid getting caught. It also teaches that might makes right, which brings us back to the Prussian template we have already condemned.

Now, concerns about disciplining children presume that discipline is about forcing them to change. Instead, you should focus on cultivating self-discipline as their role model. A body builder does not get strong by having his trainer throw weights at him. He is coached, advised, and encouraged—he picks those weights up himself. The path to mastery is internal.

## What Discipline Really Should Be

Our definition of discipline has nothing to do with punishment or spanking. Discipline means to impart knowledge and skill, not punishment and control. Discipline is effectively facilitated by having a strong bond with the child—one of trust, honesty, and consistency. Discipline is a structure of bringing the emotional, physical, social, and intellectual maturity of the child through their developmental levels and needs without detrimental stress.

Discipline is a skill that is acquired by practice. Practice is used to develop skills—often through trial and error. Encouragement, rather than discouragement, serves this journey. Shaming and/or negative enforcement is counterproductive and can threaten the parent-child bond that is necessary for the child to achieve mastery. Children must be made aware that mistakes are not necessarily negative and are not met with anger or shaming, but with understanding and instruction as mistakes are an integral and inseparable part of learning new skills.

The true meaning of discipline is "regular practice toward mastery." Most children are unable to develop it—first and foremost because their families offer no such examples. "Disciplining" children is what parents with little to no self-discipline, self-restraint, and ability to self-soothe do to their children. Instead, you need to model self-discipline.

If we haven't mastered self-discipline, how can we guide our children? Children naturally seek to model the behavior of those they are bonded to. The child's trust needs to be 100 percent bonded to parents, not peers. Spanking, punishing, and forcing children into specific behaviors that please parents push them toward modeling the dysfunction of their other relationships, like their peers.

You are the model or template of "acceptable" behavior for your child. What then are you modeling with yelling, manipulating, and hitting? Are you not teaching that "might makes right" and that it's OK to bully others? This is why children bully and why children with bossy parents are bossy with their peers. Be the model of virtue in practice—genuine, consistent, patient, and understanding. You will then see these virtues mirrored back to you by your children. An easy way to remember is that loving relationships do not require aggression. Dr. Gabor Mate, the renowned Canadian physician, author, specialist in childhood development, addiction, trauma, and mental health, proposed another succinct way to view discipline:

> If you want to discipline your kids, make them your disciples. A disciple is someone who is not afraid of you. A disciple is someone who loves you and wants to belong to you and follow you. Discipline is the very opposite of punishment.[34]

For all these reasons, the approach to use is to practice patience, empathy, and understanding. These are what create a positive impact on children and provide them the right template to copy.

## We Need to Make More Mistakes—and Feel Good about Them!

Mistakes are absolutely necessary to the learning process and discovery— they are the doorway to innovation. Never treat your children's mistakes as some sort of character flaw. Children don't want to make mistakes just as adults don't like to make mistakes. The difference is, however, that adults have the advantage of long-term experience to witness how mistakes have played out in their lives. Children don't have this advantage and are prone to internalizing mistakes as personal failures. We need to guide them to see mistakes as information and feedback and not as a path to parental disappointment or wrath. Just like a video game, in which skill levels and trials are a fun and challenging part of game play, so we parents can make "leveling

---

34  Maté, Gabor. Instagram, April 5, 2022. https://www.google.com/url?q=https://www.instagram.com/p/Cb_HVBeu5fm/?utm_source%3Dig_web_copy_link&sa=D&source=docs&ust=1682011936656945&usg=AOvVaw0KpOaG-z0ie9b7Dmsuhtxsm.

up" an important discovery process. Mistakes are crucial and necessary in any attempt at learning a new skill. Practice is used to develop skills through trial and error. Encouragement, not discouragement, serves this journey. Shaming or negative reinforcement is counterproductive and threatens the parent-child bond necessary to achieve maturity and agency.

## Parents are the Template, for Good or Bad

If you haven't yet mastered basic social dynamics and self-reflection but rely on authority alone as a parent, there will inevitably be conflict. Authoritarian parenting will demand obedience based on the use of force or "consequences." Is that the template you want your children to mirror back to you? How about to their children? Aren't we trying to break free of this model in the public schools? We must master conflict resolution in order to help children overcome their own conflicts through their practice of seeing how you manage conflict. This not only includes interpersonal conflicts but also work-related general stressors, emergency situations, marital issues, and any other behavior they will pick up—they will pick it all up, good and bad. If it works, they will adopt it. Unfortunately, just because something works and is successful doesn't mean it is good, social, healthy, moral, or honorable.

Children model successful strategies—if it works to get the outcome they want, it must be good, right? This includes the parental models of threats, punishments, striking, and bribes, which are forms of manipulation that elevate desired outcomes above children's development and their relationships with their parents. But that's not the only source of what your child's developing brain will evaluate. They will adopt social strategies from their peers—have you developed the strong parental bonds of trust that can successfully overwrite the social malware of their peers? Of strangers? Of society?

If you have daughters, know that modeling antisocial behaviors such as threats, violence, and bribes prepares them to seek the familiar in their partners. That's why some girls are attracted to "bad boys." Chances are that a bad boy endured similar dysfunctional, isolating experiences as a child.

And now he believes that the way to show love is with violence, coercion, punishment, and mixed messages.

When the parent-child relationship is healthy, positive, and strong, the parents are ready to teach anything and the children are ready to learn from them. So how do we create nurturing, strengthening, empowering relationships? What do we need to be aware of that we're not already?

People ask me, "What is a good curriculum?" I always answer, "Curriculum is like a hand tool. It's only as good as the person wielding it." The truth is that the parent-child relationship will make or break any methodology or teaching approach. To succeed, the parent also needs a "philosophy of teaching" that doesn't just cover academics but can be applied to all learning. So, with a good parent-child relationship understood, let us now begin to build our philosophy and cover the holy grail of education—motivation.

# CHAPTER 3

# Guiding Your Child's Natural Learning & Motivation

So far, we've established that children don't need the traditional school system, whether outside or inside the home. There's no need to recreate a typical schoolroom, class schedule, or even subjects from the government schools at home.

All learning can happen the same way it happened before your child reached kindergarten age: through parenting. Before children reach school age, parents are natural observers, seeing where their children are, what their natural strengths are, and how they're beginning to teach themselves.

Learning your family's values is the same as learning any other skill, as we've established. It's the same with learning mathematics or learning a second (or third!) language. As long as the environment at home is peaceful, low stress, and conducive to learning and self-teaching, children can learn anything.

Finally, with a flourishing relationship, you can help your children guide their own learning. Here's what that can look like.

# Provide the Space and Opportunities for Children to Discover Themselves

Before you guide your children in a multitude of directions, like enrolling them in every extracurricular activity, have you asked yourself why you are choosing these paths? Are all these directions even wanted by the child?

Depending on age and where children are in their developmental stage, they will sometimes seek more social interactions, and at other times, they will seek more private time to think for themselves. Allowing children to practice that freedom to choose and respecting it will minimize the conflicts and stress that may arise in the home.

Whether it's sports, music, arts, clubs, hobbies, or any other skill or activity that would be considered extracurricular, it is true that a parent doesn't experience much conflict with their children regarding the things they already enjoy doing. The child is already self-motivated and determined to engage in those activities; they are having a great time. A parent can in a very creative way enhance those activities, help children get more out of them, and even cross-reference/intertwine traditional subjects like math, science, and history into the mix.

How so?

Let us give you an example. Let's say a young boy likes to play baseball but is struggling with batting and hand-eye coordination. He wants to improve and become a more valuable player to his team because he would enjoy it even more that way. What can a parent do? A parent can suggest some more one-on-one practice. Mathematics can be introduced with a table, on which they can keep track of how much practice he does and the outcomes of the practice. How many times the boy bats a day while practicing gets recorded. How many successes were there? Then he can determine if there's something else that needs to be done to improve. Science can be introduced by showing a video that explains hand-eye coordination and then shows the correct posture for swinging with a bat. While getting better in batting practice, the child may ask, "Am I the only one who struggles with this?" The parent can remind their son that many players actually start that way. History can be introduced with a video or book that shows all the baseball players and their struggles. The records can show how some players didn't play that great one year, and then in another year, they were exceptionally amazing. The child may inquire about what it might have been like to be a professional baseball player. English can be introduced by reading a novel or even an autobiography of a famous baseball player. And that doesn't even begin to cover all the other questions that a child may have while on his journey of mastering his interest. You must seize these opportunities in a very natural way and show him how to use academics for learning and how this information can be used in everyday life. Show him how to research information and how to acquire and use the knowledge to master concepts and skills.

Consider another example. All children love the holidays because of the fun, festive ambience they bring. Families come together year after year to make memories. Make the most of that. You can cook or bake together, and you can cover several lessons in home economics. Children are naturally curious and want to know why holidays are celebrated. You can introduce the history of the holidays by reading about them or watching documentaries. At this point, you can bring more meaning to why these get celebrated and show the value and importance of traditions and culture. You can throw in arts-and-crafts activities and play games, and this will naturally encourage the children to master many skills and concepts. And most importantly, they are developing fond memories of their childhood, and they will remember the positivity and enjoyment of learning together. Again, a parent demonstrates the skills necessary to research and learn about something new in a warm and pleasant environment. You're also teaching the value and importance of spending time with family, which the children will continue to practice on their own.

Instead of making children learn subjects separately from lectures, textbooks, and tests, infuse those subjects into what the children already enjoy. That's how we go about life, after all. This builds on the Observation Pillar (which we will discuss later) —as you observe your child, you are uniquely capable of watching their interests develop and steering learning toward those interests.

Do you have a child interested in, say, Japanese mythology? They can begin learning Japanese! It's so natural to learn that way, but most parenting happens on the surface; there's little depth to understanding the child as a person, as a thinking individual.

Now consider a difficult subject all children are supposed to learn—math. Our daughter once asked us, "Why are graphs important?" We answered, predictably, "Algorithms." They're written to guide many different things, like advertising. If someone clicks on a certain type of ad often, trends result in predictability. The more complex, the better the predictability. Having a model of predictability is as essential to human survival today as it was thousands of years ago, when hunters threw spears at running gazelles. The hunter quickly learned to throw the spear *not* at the gazelle, but where it was *going to be.* Better predictability lends itself to predicting the future. The Greeks had a different name for it, as we told our daughter. The Greeks called it *prophecy.* The Oracle of Delphi was famous for accurate and precise foretelling of future events. All this intertwining and connection from math to ancient man to advertising to algorithms to ancient Greece opened our daughter's mind. She said, "I can learn math and predict the future!" Learning advanced mathematics was something she wanted to do because of how we taught her. We then told her, "History is the past—what worked and what didn't, English is about effective self-expression, and math predicts the future."

Do you notice what's happening here? We're focusing on how these subjects are useful for the child. It's going beyond teaching subjects within or outside a child's interests. It's now showing what's in it for them.

## "What's in It for Me?" The Key to Motivation and Self-Learning

In the previous chapter, we talked about a peaceful, noncoercive learning environment. Schools, and even some homeschools, are violent, coercive learning environments, which are not conducive to learning. The problem with having an annual curriculum, semester-based subjects, daily required lessons, lesson plans covering mandatory tests, and so on is that these are fundamentally coercive. In other words, the child has to, and when the child has to, they no longer *want* to.

The only way that coercion works is when the child wants to do something of their own free will—they actually *want* to complete the algebra textbook. They may even tell you that they want to take a couple of weeks on their own to complete an entire textbook or workbook that children are usually forced to complete over three months in a regular school.

Children are like magnets. If you push them, they're pushed away. Pull with persuasion, and they're pulled in. This leads us to the idea of personal agency, which is the philosopher's stone of motivation. Let's state that again, agency is the philosopher's stone of motivation—and it's true for children as well as adults.

*Agency* (psychological definition): the degree to which an individual has the ability to make decisions about their life. To have agency means to have control or the feeling of control over your life and the decisions you make.

Let's talk about motivation in the context of agency. The common definition of *motivation* is the impetus that gives purpose or reason to a behavior. That impetus is always a force and is always external. There is no external motivation that is not inherently classified as either the use of force or the use of persuasion. It is either the club or the carrot, a pointed gun or a logical appeal, armies crossing borders or trade—a positive versus negative dichotomy. In other words, we are either incentivizing with rewards, or we are disincentivizing with punishment.

We need to scrap the idea of an intrinsic-versus-extrinsic motivation model—it doesn't exist, or at least, the behaviorist model of Ivan Pavlov and B. F. Skinner (and others) is of limited use for humans. Conditioning observations in animal training do show results on a wide scale, but the human mind is far more complex. Operant conditioning, with its positive and negative reinforcements and classical conditioning of modifying an existing behavior, does not affect learning in humans. We are far less susceptible to these enforcers and stimuli than our nonhuman counterparts. Why? The simple answer I propose for why we are less susceptible is that we recognize when we are being manipulated or "played," and that breaks trust.

So ditch the manipulative parenting and teaching model of the behaviorists.[35] We have a better model for you.

We have been taught in our universities that intrinsic motivation comes from a natural or inherent enjoyment of the activity, and external motivation is incentivized from an outside source. But how, then, do we explain what motivates a child to play or read for hours on their own? Is there a threat or treat in this equation? If impetus is force or even persuasion, where is that inner dialogue? Where does a sense of agency coincide with motivation?

Professor Steven Reiss at Ohio State University proposed the sixteen basic desires theory of motivation.

The sixteen distinct needs fulfillments that drive us to everything we want in life include:

1. Acceptance, the need to be appreciated

2. Curiosity, the need to gain knowledge

3. Eating, the need for food

4. Family, the need to take care of offspring

5. Honor, the need to be faithful to the values of the ethnic group, family, or clan

6. Idealism, the need for justice

7. Independence, the need to be distinct and self-reliant

8. Order, the need for prepared, established, and conventional environments

9. Physical activity, the need for working out the body

10. Power, the need for control of will

11. Romance, the need for mating (sexual intimacy)

12. Saving, the need to accumulate something

---

35  Scott H. Kollins, M. Christopher Newland, and Thomas S. Critchfield, "Human Sensitivity to Reinforcement in Operant Choice: How Much Do Consequences Matter?" Psychonomic Bulletin & Review 4 (1997): 208–220, https://doi.org/10.3758/BF03209395.

13. Social contact, the need for relationship with others

14. Social status, the need for social significance

15. Tranquility, the need to be secure and protected

16. Vengeance, the need to strike back against another person

Working with homeschool parents and their children has taught us that all sixteen desires can be summarized into two—yes, only two. Together, these cover the entirety of self-motivation. And they are:

1. The *freedom* to access one's own imagination and creativity

2. The *ability* to act on one's own imagination and creativity

This is in no way to disrespect Professor Reiss's work—he's spot on. However, consider how even the worst procrastinator will have a hobby they will spend hours on and learn about—even if that is a video game. If it enlightens imagination and creativity, it motivates. This is precisely the same formula for and definition of agency: that is, of being free to make rational decisions and to ask oneself, *Do I have the ability to control decisions? Can I do it? Can I own it?*

Having high agency implies that an individual is one who desires, makes plans, and carries out their actions. Having low agency is hallmarked by an individual's dissociation or an ambiguity between himself and the things they do or have done.

In child development, low agency is commonly associated with an abusive environment—the harsher the environment, the lower the agency developed. Operationally, low agency in an abusive household can be a survival mechanism. It makes no sense to always be confronting a harsh caregiver who dictates everything you do—it's easier to just go along with what they tell you to do. The result of this is that we are conditioned to do as we are told. We are stripped of a developmental stage when we start to practice agency, and yet we are told to be responsible. Creativity and imagination that lead to success do not develop in a high-stress, abusive dynamic. They can take a more personally destructive turn—escapism.

We also know that an abusive environment affects brain development: specifically, the posterior parietal cortex as it is responsible for self-recognition. If you are not homeschooling, you are fighting for your child's model of what is true and what is good and for their creativity. Public (and some private) schools are not about education. They are about stress compliance: i.e., obedience training. Homeschooling, on the other hand, can be used to develop children's agency, individual ability, and initiative.

So how do you "pull" your children toward learning and persuade them to want to apply themselves academically? Think about the saying "The apple doesn't fall far from the tree." The brain wants models of success, a.k.a. mimicry. If your child sees you as a living example of "What's in it for me?" they'll want that. We saw a father and son running together recently. The father was most likely a runner years before the child was even born and set an example for the son to imitate. The son sees his father running, and that motivates him to take it up. That's the power of mimesis. By a parent's action of establishing a successful habit, they model the habit. Children want to be good at things. They inherently love competition—and winning. And if there's a close bond, you're already your child's hero. Your children will do as you model, for better or worse.

For instance, when we taught our daughter to play Yahtzee®, she had a young mind and emotions but showed a desire to play. We let her win a lot. Imagine if we'd played our hardest. She'd never win, and it wouldn't be fun. Victory and fun are the "What's in it for me?" We had to then show her how to win and to lose—modeling graceful winning and losing. We also taught her that both chance and skill are involved in any game, and you choose the game accordingly. If it's mostly chance, like Go Fish, it's easy for a child to win. But you gauge what games to play by chance and strategy. But the "What's in it for me?" is always the same—winning. You have to give your child a taste of success. That's why, in the Montessori method, it is advised not trying anything too challenging too early. When children fail, they may not be mentally prepared and thus are easily discouraged and abandon the idea of trying again. However, when the task is just challenging enough or relatively easy, then they want to continue to try, and they will even start challenging themselves simply because they achieved a goal presented to them. It is about maintaining that confidence in children that allows them to continue to discover and learn. Interestingly enough, this is exactly how video game makers keep players engaged in their games.

Here's another example. Our daughter got interested in chess because I (Jonathan) told her a story. I used to go to Starbucks a few times a week, and there was often a physics professor I'd catch up with. He liked to play chess. It turned out he was a bona fide chess master, and he'd invite me to play. Of course I lost, but he invited me to play several more times. I kept losing until, finally, I beat him. And he was such a curmudgeon that he almost threw the pieces. But I beat him once, and that was enough for me. After that, he kept asking me to play again. I always declined because I'd reached the level I wanted to. My daughter thought that was such an entertaining story that I, her father, beat a chess master and wouldn't give him the time of day for a rematch. She thought that was funny. So she said, "I would love to learn to play chess."

It is not uncommon for parents to be concerned that if they don't force their child to learn reading, writing, and mathematics, they won't want to learn. We hear ADHD brought up often. Parents will say, "But my child won't sit and pay attention," yet their child plays video games with complex rules, moves, stats, and activities for hours. We are not disparaging the challenges of neurodivergent children, but can we make a creative connection for the child that solves this? Are we going to write off these challenges and throw our hands up in learned helplessness under the guise of a diagnosis? Did you know that ADHD may have helped our hunter-gatherer ancestors survive?[36] Can we bring this knowledge into our method of interacting with our ADHD children? Maybe bringing the child's interests into what they are learning is key for them to want to focus and concentrate. Maybe we follow the child, observe and create an environment where they can thrive because sometimes you have to see where their interests take them.

Strategize. Figure out the things your child is into, or just ask them and let them pontificate about their favorite things. Listen intently. Does your child like Batman? What about a Batman graphic novel? Do they like to play video games? What about an age-appropriate computer game that teaches math? Whatever the child may hesitate to learn is the result of not seeing the "What's in it for me?" regarding what you want them to learn. Bring those interests into the learning plan, and the resistance drops.

---

36   Goldman, Laura, Dana Robinson, and Brian Krans. "ADHD and Evolution: Were Hyperactive Hunter-Gatherers Better Adapted Than Their Peers?" Healthline, March 15, 2021. https://www.healthline.com/health/adhd/evolution#How-to-use-ADHD-to-your-advantage.

Figure out other ways to learn about your child's interests. Is your child hands on? Get them a sample of pond water, glass slides, and a twenty-dollar microscope. Do they love reading? Get a comic book covering a period of US history they're interested in. What about an audiobook? This is especially helpful for children with disabilities, for whom traditional schooling pressures are even worse. It's possible for some of these skills to come later. The good news is that they will master them eventually.

What would help the child most with his independence is reading, and it's important to model the world of books early on. We cannot emphasize enough how important this is—a child who can read is a child who can teach himself anything. The earlier this goal is learned, the better off he is.

## Implementing the Joy of Reading at Home

Our daughter began reading her first words at ten months old. She never had the terrible twos because she could understand the world around her and communicate. When children feel like they are not understood and are struggling, they get frustrated. This frustration is oftentimes outwardly displayed as tantrums or "acting out"—this is about the ability to communicate. This frustration would be the same if you as an adult have a problem communicating in a foreign country, and you have to resort to "acting out" what you want to say. As parents we must provide the tools of communication, understand what is being said, and make the connection to our children that we understand, and not punish them for their inability to communicate.

When our daughter was three, we were driving on the freeway, and she said, "Daddy, you're not supposed to cross the white lines." How? "I read the sign back there." Later, she reminded me, "Your exit is coming up." She was like a small human GPS. She acquired a skill that made her useful so she could contribute to her family and feel valuable. When a child is better able to communicate with you and their siblings and make sense of the world, they feel more at ease.

The utmost necessary skill that parents should implement in their home is reading. Families should be reading all the time. Children should be read to often, even every day. Reading should be presented as something pleasant that is very much enjoyed. Why? We need to help guide children into learning that books are the windows and doors to infinite knowledge and enjoyment. This is the key to future independence. Whether it is to gain knowledge in subjects of interest or to spend a wonderful time being entertained with imagination, books bring meaning and value to our lives. Children need input; reading fun, interesting things is an input that helps them inquire about and engage with the world around them.

Our minds need to be exercised to achieve that sense of fulfillment. We don't consider ourselves complete until we have used our minds to conquer something amazing. When a family reads a lot together, children get the sense that this is something natural and necessary that is done every day, like brushing their teeth. Children will emulate what parents do because we are providing that successful template for them. Eventually, children will be reading on their own, and they will unlock the magic. They start acquiring their own knowledge on whatever subject interests them. They could be reading and understanding the periodic table in their younger years without having to wait for an adult to present chemistry when they are high school age. Children can master many concepts just by reading. When they love reading, you can expect them to guide their own learning. Just remember, let their skill of reading mature *before* screens, or else you will inhibit their mastery and joy of reading. Delay electronics, screens, and flashy movies as long as you can. As much as it pains me to say it, books cannot compete with the mental mind candy of electronics.

And don't forget documentaries (one of the few screen exceptions). They can be a helpful way to ease children into new subjects they might want to learn more about by reading. Get into their brain and get curious. What will they think is fun or interesting? If it's fun or interesting, they'll want to connect the dots. They can begin to do that on their own—if they can read.

Next, let's put these new skills we have just learned into a usable structure and method—a pedagogy.

## The Three Pillars of Homeschooling Pedagogy

*Pedagogy* is a big word, but you don't need to be an academic to understand it. Pedagogy is simply a theory of methods and practices of and approaches to teaching. It's how we examine, understand, and categorize learning styles through all age groups throughout history and even across cultures and civilizations. Pedagogy crosses over psychology, anthropology, and even brain development and genetics. A parent could spend years studying the extent and nuance of all that pedagogy has to offer, but who has the time? Well, we do!

We have developed the Three Pillars of Homeschooling Pedagogy that shows us not just *what* our children need to learn but *how* we ought to teach them.

This pedagogy provides the parent a framework that ensures that the child's natural love of learning is not destroyed. It is the tool that promotes agency since it relies on principles and feedback and not on guilt and coercion. And finally, it fosters, promotes, and helps internalize meaning and purpose in the child.

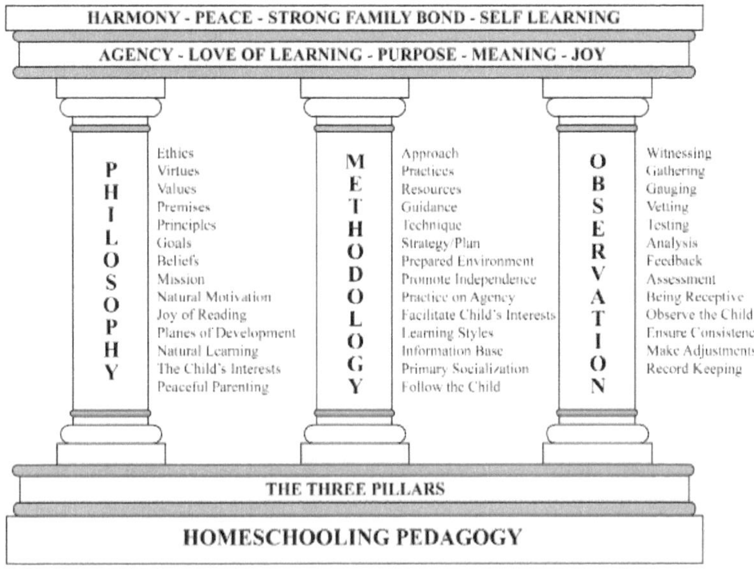


When a parent is engaged with the Three Pillars, the child will feel it—to them, it feels like the parent is participating warmly and being in-the-moment with the child. Remember, pedagogy is about teaching, and we redefine teaching in a homeschooling context as simply . . . parenting. It's just like what you've already been doing all these years with your children.

So with this pedagogy, once you learn the three pillars, it will provide you a firm foundation for *how* you will lovingly, peacefully, noncoercively teach your children how to teach themselves what they need to learn to become functional, valuable members of society.

Are you ready? Let's begin.

## The First Pedagogy Pillar: Philosophy

Nobody can get anywhere in life without a way to make sense of the world. Philosophy is that vehicle. Your family—you—need philosophy. What is it? We define philosophy as the code of values that make a person who they are, what they know to be true, and why they believe it. It's the fundamental view of how a person can make sense of reality and develop standards of conduct. Philosophy also provides your family a foundation for consistency, objectivity, and functionality regardless of the situation.

Philosophy is divided into metaphysics, epistemology, and ethics. Putting it in everyday terms, philosophy is the study of what is *real* (metaphysics), what is *true* (epistemology), and what is *good* (ethics). We already have some framework in our lives to sort this out, but many parents have trouble articulating to their children *why* they believe or know certain things to be good or bad; *how* to think about new information; or, when faced with injustice, *what* to do that will not contradict their values and judgments.

Once you can employ the cognitive tool of philosophy, you can navigate your own mind and worldview looking for inconsistencies and contradictions to strengthen your values and beliefs about the world around you. After that, you will be able to quickly process any new ideas, concepts, or systems that cross your path—such as a new curriculum, history textbook, or homeschooling method. You will be able to answer:

- How old or new resources align with your family's values
- How to spot and evaluate detrimental developmental inputs (negative influences)
- How to articulate your family's goals and mission for homeschooling

- How to analyze and break down the information or skills being taught in the resources—what is of value, what is necessary, and what can be discarded

Homeschoolers are not burdened with the constant demand of one-size-fits-all education, so we have it easy relative to public and even private school teachers. We have only our children to teach. This also means we have home field advantage, meaning we don't have to be multicultural, multi-value, diverse, or even inclusive in the progressive sense. Parents are free to teach the values, morals, culture, ancestry, worldview, creed, or religion that is important to them. There are no stressed environments or forced associations; homeschoolers are at home with their loving parents.

Parents need to have the proper philosophy of education and understand how learning happens and how their own children learn. The learning experience needs to be interesting and fun, not forced. Parents can implement what was learned earlier in the chapters regarding peaceful parenting, making mistakes, discovery, motivation, agency, being a good model, "What's in it for me?" and early reading. Children should love learning, and when we include these values and virtues through philosophy, children learn more naturally. Incorporating certain conditions in their homes will also instill the love of learning such as:

- Providing freedom for children to choose what they want to learn
- Providing a stress-free home and learning environment
- Allowing children to exercise independence and agency
- Providing a prepared environment aligned with their development stage
- Providing an ambience where it is interesting, fun, and exciting to learn all the time

So how do you create an easygoing environment optimized for learning in a fun way? Well, learning can happen anytime, so seize teaching opportunities when children are already excited. Creating a peaceful and stress-free environment helps children maintain a positive attitude toward life. Help them feel like valuable members of the family by allowing them to have a voice—to participate in conversations—and letting them help you when they offer and then thanking them. Make the environment at home optimal for fun, interesting, and independent learning for the children appropriate to their development stages. With these in place, they will be more apt to want to learn about anything and, more importantly, to want to learn from you, their parents.

In the home, we need to adopt what Maria Montessori developed and called, The Prepared Environment and it must evolve with the child as they progress through the developmental stages. The main elements in the prepared environment should include:

- A large space or several small spaces that are mainly for the child's use
- Ergonomic furniture sized for a growing child
- A cheerful and happy ambience
- Educational materials appropriate for the child's level of development
- Hands-on learning kits
- Child-accessible shelves to hold the educational materials
- Fun and creative activities that the child can work on independently
- Activities that foster imagination and creativity
- Learning materials that promote self-correction
- Freedom of movement (floor space, comfortable sofa or chair, table and chairs, etc.)
- Beautiful arrangement and organization
- A variety of items on rotation that always provide something new to discover
- A safe setting according to the age of the child
- Different means of learning the same lesson to promote freedom of choice
- The independence to function without parents present
- Elements from outside brought into the classroom

The Prepared Environment is a concept of a designed and carefully structured learning environment where learning materials, room layout, accessibility, and aesthetics promote and facilitate a child's natural curiosity. All learning materials have a purpose and a goal to build lessons that meet the needs of the child's development stages. Hence, these materials are not "toys" as the untrained eye might assume, but meet the core purpose of the Prepared Environment—to build the child's ability and courage to take charge of their own learning, exploration, self-expression, discovery, agency, and independence.

We include the Prepared Environment as part of the first pillar as it is a philosophical basis for this new approach. Understanding the impact the environment has on the children's natural inclination towards learning allows you to create an optimal space where you can shepherd and guide their learning to their own potential. You will know when the environment is prepared correctly when children naturally want to spend time there, and they are having a good time learning independently, even when you are not in there with them.

## The Second Pedagogy Pillar: Methodology

Let's say you are ready to start homeschooling. You may have some idea as to what to do and what you are going to teach and even how to teach it—all of which is a rough "method" that you are going to employ. What happens next? Do you follow what you vaguely remember from your own school experience? Do you know what your child's learning style is? What development stage are they in? What type of homeschooling are you going to employ? Unschooling? Charlotte Mason? Classical? Eclectic?

When we say methodology is part of homeschooling pedagogy, we mean that it includes the specifics of the methods, plans, best practices, procedures, prepared environment, resources, textbooks, trips, and all other materials—that it has a purpose and a goal, and it aligns with and promotes the first pillar of philosophy—your family's values. Methodology is your game plan, and the goals of your methods must be something you can write down and articulate. They must be shared with your family members so that everyone has an idea of what will be happening in the home. How you will implement the schedules, record keeping, planning, transcripts, and calendars are also part of this pillar.

Methodology means the specific approach for delivering information and lessons. It outlines how to prepare the environment for optimal learning. You can refine the resources (information) used and how to best present them to the children. You figure out how to keep them excited about learning and allow them to become independent so that they can continue learning without you being present. Methodology is the incorporation of best-chosen practices that encourage children to have fun and learning goals that promote self-motivation and agency with the ultimate goal of independent work.

For example, if you want to teach counting, then have several options of accessible, hands-on materials that the child can use to practice counting. You can even make them holiday or season themed if you think that would appeal to the child. If you think the child would be interested in learning about animals that live in the ocean, then plan a field trip to the aquarium—anything that gets them excited about learning more. Coupling that with visits to the library to get books on their areas of interest will get them to want to read about them. Learning becomes effortless when you take advantage of the opportunities and choices presented to the children. Be creative, smart, clever, and flexible when implementing methodology. Follow the child.

Remember, methodology is developed by a solid, non-contradictory philosophy and is dependent on this philosophy for stability. You cannot support a child's love of learning and agency without all three pillars, but the dynamic interaction between methodology and philosophy will be the most challenging for the parent. How do I assure the balance between these two pillars? That is found in the pillar of Observation.

## The Third Pedagogy Pillar: Observation

The great pedagogical observer was Dr. Maria Montessori. Her analytical and thorough scientific observations on how children learn impressed the world and reached across disciplines. Because of her observations, she was able to educate children who had been considered unteachable, labeled as "idiots," and institutionalized. She taught these children to read and write and pass the standard aptitude tests at levels comparable to their public school contemporaries, her observations produced her methodology—the Montessori method. As Maria Montessori said, "Scientific observation then has established that education is not what the teacher gives; education is a natural process spontaneously carried out by the human individual and is acquired not by listening to words but by experiences upon the environment."[37]

Observers, however, are not mere watchers with some *Star Trek*–style prime directive of noninterference. The observation is purpose-driven to assess learning stages, interests, bursts of imagination, and changes of attention. Observation is not limited to homeschooling time—it's all the time. Observation is information gathering for the parent to optimize not just learning but all aspects of parenting. Get to know the child—find out what their preferences are and what gets them excited. Learn how the child responds to the academic subjects and find out their strengths and weaknesses. Observe their actions, reactions, facial expressions, and body language. When Montessori said, "Follow the child, but follow them as their leader," this was the depth of the observation she meant. Montessori further explained, "[Children] will show you what they need to do, what they need to develop in themselves, and what area they need to be challenged in."[38]

Parents are the guides and mentors of children. Their prime directive is to prepare them for the future with a level of mental, emotional, physical maturity, and agency so they can not only navigate but also thrive during both uncertainty and opportunity. Through observation, parents can assess whether enough opportunities were presented for optimal learning. They find out whether the prepared environment was successful or not and figure out what tweaking needs to be done. Sometimes it is observed that the philosophy was not implemented fully, and hence, conflict arose in the household. The practice of observation throughout the child's learning experience allows parents to honestly assess not just the results of the children but also the effectiveness of their own efforts. In the end, it is for

37  Paula K. Greene, "Dear Maria Montessori," Kappa Delta Pi Record (Summer 2005): 164–166, https://files.eric.ed.gov/fulltext/EJ724891.pdf.

38  Paula K. Greene, "Dear Maria Montessori," Kappa Delta Pi Record (Summer 2005): 164–166, https://files.eric.ed.gov/fulltext/EJ724891.pdf.

the children's sake, and every parent wants their children to be happy and content when they are learning.

To summarize, you can teach anything in the homeschool because the world is the classroom, and society as a whole is the children's classmate. Parents guide their children, so it's their job to teach them how to navigate and become experts.

There are times when a parent feels intimidated because of a lack of knowledge or inexperience teaching; then maybe the parent and the child should be students together. Becoming classmates creates opportunities to strengthen the parent-child bond. Children really love to learn, not only *from* their parents but also *with* their parents. So don't think you have to acquire mastery before introducing information or skills to your children.

You should now be beginning to realize that your children don't need school; they need you and everything you can offer them. Once you start treating them as fellow human beings, you allow your relationship to blossom. It puts an end to the menial treatment of the Prussian model of schooling.

Now, as we begin to wrap up this chapter, you may be facing nagging questions such as, "Great. I love how easy and seamless it can be in everyday life to inspire my child to want to learn, even to want to teach themselves. But how much should my child have learned already? Are they ahead? Behind? How much should they be self-taught, and how often should I be right beside them like an instructor or a tutor?"

You may also be thinking, *Oh no! My kid is behind. Now what?* These are simple questions that have satisfying yet complex answers, which we'll reveal in the next chapter. For now, though, we'd like to shoot back at that question with a question.

*My kid is behind,* you might worry. What we say is, "Behind what, exactly?"

CHAPTER 4

# What if Your Kid Falls Behind?

Remember, measurements used in the school system like grades, assignments, and tests are not good metrics for success in life. They just show how well children's temporary memories and memorization in general work. Typically, right after the assignments and tests are completed the information gets mentally discarded—forgotten as soon as the new assignments and tests get assigned. Therefore, not all the information taught in schools has been learned because it hasn't been permanently absorbed—subjects and concepts are then not actually mastered by the children. Mastery occurs when the information or skill stays with you for life and has become either meaningful or useful to you.

To understand what homeschooling accomplishes, focus on mastery rather than misguided measurements of "learning." To put your mind at ease, remember the unique benefits homeschooling provides—benefits no other form of schooling can offer. In your homeschool, you can give your children:

1. **True mastery of the information and skills they learn.** You and your children decide how much learning is enough for the level of

mastery they want to achieve: familiarity (beginner), proficiency (intermediate), or mastery (advanced).

2. **Student-led pace of learning.** It's usually slow going when something new is first introduced. Then when it's grasped, the pace picks up quickly.

3. **Independence, confidence, and courage.** By being in control of their present and future, your kid can be exceptional in their own unique way.

4. **Enjoyable learning.** This is what really provides the freedom to succeed in life. If learning isn't a hang-up or an unpleasant experience, then learning will continue forever, effortlessly; this is true power and success.

5. **Self-teaching and opportunities to teach others.** By learning to be in control of their learning, children become unstoppable lifelong learners of anything. They'll learn so well that it won't be long before they can competently teach others.

6. **Freedom to discover aha moments of knowing what they want to do.** When children know themselves and have the freedom to pursue their interests, they discover much sooner what they want to do with their lives. They form clear pictures of what they want to pursue, making it easier for them to master the subject matter that matches the future they want. All of a sudden, the academics needed for that future are no longer hurdles but become fun challenges your kid decides to overcome and succeed at.

7. **Freedom to choose the resources that best suit their interests.** In the beginning, you can introduce all the available options for learning to your kid. Eventually, as they discover the specifics of what they enjoy learning and what they will want to pursue in life, they can choose the resources (books, videos, instructors, etc.) that best align with their desires.

8. **Preparation for life and a path to success.** With the gained independence and agency, children learn what they need to know to benefit their future, and they learn to adjust their learning based on that. They understand that learning happens 24-7 and know how well to access the resources necessary to master what they need to learn.

# Teach to Mastery—Not to a Grade

Grades are a poor metric for testing subject knowledge. At best, grades are a general indicator of current familiarity with a subject. One thing that grades do well is to create an artificial social hierarchy and a reinforcement of negative self-esteem. This kills motivation. It invokes social shame as papers and tests are handed back. Imagine not needing any of that stress. Teaching to mastery means you know when you know something, and you know when your kid knows something. Can you still give a test to be sure? Yes, if you think it's necessary—but that's for you and your child to decide.

Here's how it works. When your kid is mastering a new skill or subject, there are three basic levels of knowledge:

1. Familiarity

2. Proficiency

3. Mastery

*Familiarity* implies a modest amount of experience. Some teenagers might be familiar with the controls of a car (e.g., they know the difference between the brake pedal and the gas pedal, they know how to steer and use turn signals, etc.). They may even have some driving experience, but by no means would they be considered experts—not if they are merely familiar with driving.

*Proficiency* implies a sufficient level of expertise, to the point at which the individual is trusted to do any sort of task. Some areas might have an exam required, by which people can demonstrate their proficiencies. You must demonstrate your driving proficiency before you can obtain a driver's license.

*Mastery* implies a level of expertise beyond proficiency. An instructor at a driving school may have mastery of the skill—not only is the instructor a good driver, but they can also teach other people about the hazards of driving, safe driving habits, et cetera. They might also have had experience practicing, say, maneuvering out of a skid.

For other subjects, such as history, English, math, science, et cetera, you're evaluating one on one daily through your observation (three pillars).

The better your observation skills, the better you can assess mastery in your children. You can now ditch the grades.

*But how do I know if they're ahead or behind?* you might still wonder. The four planes of child development collectively hold your answer.

# Dr. Maria Montessori's Four Planes of Child Development

"Is my kid behind?" is a simple question with a complex but illuminating answer. First, let's rephrase the question as "What stage of development is my child at, and are they tracking to that stage?" Just like the other tools we've already mentioned, such as the three pillars, motivation, and teaching to mastery, this next tool will complete your tool kit.

Of all the models for explaining your child's development, it is perhaps Maria Montessori's four planes of child development that are the most valuable. The four planes of child development answer the question "Where is my child, and where are they supposed to be?" This helps parents make sense of what could be the root cause if their child is struggling.

The four planes are divided into infancy (zero to six years), childhood (six to twelve years), adolescence (twelve to eighteen years), and maturity (eighteen to twenty-four years). Each plane (or period) has a construction phase and a consolidation phase. The construction phase is about building the skills and elements for that plane, and the consolidation phase is about refining and honing those skills (mastery).

Through her lifetime's worth of research and observations on how children learn best, and over the last hundred years, Dr. Maria Montessori's four planes of child development still hold to be helpful and true today. The premise is that children tend to exhibit certain characteristics, needs, and natural developmental milestones that fall into four age ranges or planes.

This approach takes into consideration every aspect of the child's needs, such as physical, intellectual, social, and emotional. When educating your children, the planes let you identify where they belong.

## THE FOUR PLANES OF DEVELOPMENT

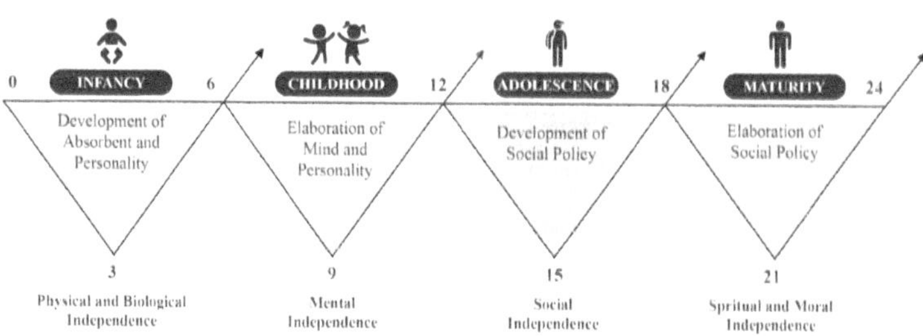


This means you're better able to understand why your child is struggling in certain areas and are therefore better able to help them. You can guide them in choosing resources and materials to best learn certain subjects, help them decide what subjects to discuss, and determine how to prepare your environment for healthy development and optimal learning. While each child is unique, these planes describe the typical patterns in brain development and will reveal the readiness of the child to learn something in particular.

Within the planes of development, Dr. Montessori discusses progression, regression, pinnacle, and sensitive periods. These are the patterns of growth that children journey through. In each plane, your child will exhibit a series of progressions, followed by a series of regressions. The progressions take place in the first half of each plane. Your child goes through an intense developmental change, called a "sensitive period," when they're concentrated, focused, and interested in what they're learning. These sensitive periods are windows of opportunity when a child is capable of learning certain concepts more easily and naturally than at any other time of development. As a parent, good observation skills help you focus on what your child is most interested in at any given moment so you can capitalize on it by providing more opportunities for the child to continue engaging in that interest. This is how you facilitate and enable a child's desire to pursue a skill and set goals to acquire mastery of that skill.

Each plane will also be marked by a pinnacle, which is a period when the child fully and clearly exhibits the characteristics of that particular plane of development. Then the regressions take place in the second half of each plane, when the child refines and assimilates what they learned in the first half. This means that at the end of each plane, you'll see their confidence in their mastery—commonly by their ability, willingness, and excitement to teach others—including wanting to teach you.

As a parent, be aware not only of ensuring your child is ready to learn the next sequence of skills but also of not holding them back from transitioning to the next plane. If held back, the child will show signs of a different type of regression, when they may no longer want to do certain things or they appear bored. This could be caused by an intellectual or emotional need not being met. It's important to observe the child's pace in learning so they're always able to move positively forward when ready. Stagnation affects children emotionally, and they lose confidence. The prepared environment you provide is key in helping your child stay on the path of joyful learning and have the flexibility to independently move forward at their own pace. We'll discuss each plane in more detail so you can see how they all come together. Then you'll realize just how powerful a tool it really is.

## The First Plane of Child Development, Age Zero to Six

In the first plane of development, the child is experiencing an explosion of exploration of the physical world. They use all their senses to absorb everything in their environment. They want answers to questions related to where they are, what the world is, and how things work.[39] All their needs—physical, intellectual, social, and emotional—are affected. It's typical for a four-year old to ask questions about everything to the point where some adults get annoyed! However, it's important for parents to get in touch with their inner child and join their child on that level of discovery. This is how you have fun learning together.

Prepare your environment to have easily accessible resources and materials to entice the children's curiosity, satisfy their discovery, and find answers to their questions. There should be lots of concrete materials for children to manipulate so they can repeat their experiments and come to their own conclusions.

---

39  Dempsey, Judy. Essay. In Turning Education Inside-Out: Confessions of a Montessori Principal, 8–9. Plantation, FL: J. Ross Publishing, 2017.

Children at this plane of development are often interested in nature, so learning about trees, leaves, flowers, rocks, insects, et cetera is well suited. Spending time outside and collecting items from nature can be of interest. While inside, further study of what's collected by using a magnifying glass or jeweler's loupe and reading a book associated with the specimens are fun ways to learn. It also wouldn't be unusual to have a terrarium inside the house to bring live specimens from outside, like frogs or lizards, to watch for a short period of time before setting them free in their natural habitat.

An example would be having access to an environment where they can practice art on their own and easily clean up after themselves. This teaches children many skills, including agency, by being able to practice taking care of their environment. Also, having items on rotation, with some items stored and then brought out on a routine basis allows for activities to seem new and appeal to the child again. Paying attention to what your child is interested in will prompt you on what new resources and concrete materials to bring into the environment.

Other than the typical and common understanding of the right time when to help children learn how to crawl, eat solid foods, walk, use the potty, and dress themselves, there are other sensitive periods associated with this plane of development. Learning how to balance, count, read, and write are skills that, as a parent, you will learn when to best teach them based on observing the result of that first introductory lesson. Also take into account their development of gross and fine motor skills. The cues that children give with their responses to what you introduce, combined with the direct input they give you in return, help you identify what to focus on. Children that attend state education are not going to get any such accurate guidance. You need to remember and acknowledge that every child is unique and deserves to learn at their own pace according to their healthy development with the help and guidance of their loving parents.

Another aspect of this plane of development is that children are very empathetic. They're born helpers. Their innocence and lack of experience allow them to be very emotional and especially empathetic to a parent being sad or hurt. If parents practice reciprocity and consistently show patience, understanding, kindness, and empathy to their children, the children often pick up on this and copy what is modeled. This is the opportunity where the parents can create in the child the template of what loving relationships looks like—shunning your little helpers for some perceived time constraint will crush their spirit and this one missed opportunity can echo into trust problems later on.

Children want to help others, so it's important to allow them to help you. They want to be useful members of the family—they will even try to help the family pets in whatever the child thinks is helpful, much to the pet's patient confusion. So it's important for them to learn that their help is always welcomed and valued with verbal praise and hugs. This way, they're more apt to volunteer and continue to be helpful in the later planes of development.

Lastly, some children will be more sociable than others, so it's beneficial to understand and respect where the children stand socially. The later planes of development will provide more opportunities for children to become more sociable as they mature and develop more confidence in themselves.

## The Second Plane of Child Development, Age Six to Twelve

In the second plane of development, the child is experiencing an explosion into the exploration of the *intellectual* world. They want to increase their knowledge about the world.[40] They become young versions of scientists and engineers, continuing to ask unlimited questions about every aspect of life, including the rules of society. The intelligence of the child becomes extroverted, and their imagination grows where unlimited possibilities about the world can exist.

As a parent, you need to either have the answers ready or become good at finding the resources and materials for your child to find the answers they seek. What a child at this stage wants is to be able to make sense of the cosmic order of the world by understanding how it's all connected, including the importance of our existence. This child now has a much broader outlook on life and is more open minded. When a parent engages in many conversations with their child, the parent soon learns everything the child is interested in and wants to learn more about. Those are the cues for this stage's prepared environment and information base.

---

40   Ibid.

At this stage, the parent and child can go to the library together and check out books to bring home. There are many field trip opportunities to go out and search for information and answers. Hands-on science and engineering kits are always a hit with children at this stage. Also, a parent and child can go shopping together and purchase materials for projects.

Because the child is interested in the big picture and why it's important to learn something, time lines and stories of how things began are well received. Instead of focusing on memorizing dates, children want to know how it is all connected via a time line and have a general understanding of what happened in what order. It is advantageous for a parent to teach what we think is the most important skill at this stage: how to become an independent researcher and learn about anything on their own. This is where children practice having agency on how and what they want to learn.

Another aspect of this Plane of Development is that the child will begin to recognize moral patterns and become keenly aware of moral dilemmas and perceived hypocrisy—of their parents. However, if parents have been consistent, honest, truthful, and forthright in modeling their own behavior, the child can begin to grasp nuance and discover new areas of truth and honor. Beware, however, parents are still the protectors of their children's minds, hearts, and sensibilities—Giving up too much information too soon about the world's ills and evils can create all sorts of stress in the mind of the child.

Think about our own past human history and what would be happening during this plane of development and before modern education. The end of this stage back then marked the time when older children would go on to apprenticeships and learn a trade or skill. It was also a stage when children were more mature and understood the importance of inheritance and the responsibility of taking over a family business—a responsibility one received with great honor.

That being said, children at the end of this stage (plane) should already be independent learners and starting to think about their life goals into adulthood. Parents can still suggest skills or topics that children might not seek out themselves, which can be made interesting if the parent introduces them well. Some children may want to reach out to others and socialize, especially with people who are interested in the same things. Activity and community clubs can be very popular with children who want to learn more about certain topics or skills together with other like-minded children.

Regarding academics, learning, and brain development, it is important to note that in this plane, children transition from concrete to abstract thinking and reasoning. By having all the practice in the earlier years with learning concepts via concrete materials, they're now ready to interpret concepts in their more abstract forms. They will have already built a strong foundation and can now imagine the concrete forms in their minds. Simply put, the children are prepared and confident to face and pursue greater challenges on their own.

## The Third Plane of Child Development, Age Twelve to Eighteen

In the third plane of development, the child is experiencing an explosion into the exploration of social relationships. They can experience a very dramatic and intense entrance into early adolescence, trying to understand the social relationship part of life.[41] Much time is spent in this stage processing and clarifying the child's individual identity in society. Children are now very interested in fitting in and being accepted by society, which makes them very susceptible to outside influences and propaganda.

As discussed in the earlier chapters, having a strong parent-child bond and a healthy relationship between parents and their children helps children become more confident and grounded in the values, virtues, and traditions instilled in the family. When family is far more important than outside influences, children are not swayed. Parents complain about this difficult stage in children because they seem rebellious when they question and challenge everyone and everything—this is similar to what began in the previous plane with the moral questioning, but in this current plane, it is a moral challenge. This is a quest that children are on to finalize their understanding of the rules of society and to determine where they fit in. With the skills and knowledge they've already attained in the previous planes of development, they're trying to figure out who's consistently trustworthy and who's not. They want to know who's being a hypocrite and pretending to follow the rules. They're testing who truly has values and who is a successful

---

41   Ibid.

template to follow. They want to know how far the rules can be bent and the consequences for when the rules are broken. They want to know where they are welcomed, accepted, and to feel that they truly belong.

Emotionally, children at this stage can be very challenging as their brains are being flooded with pubescent hormones and they still haven't acquired the maturity and experience in controlling their emotions as they have never experienced this intensity before. This is where parents, through their consistent demonstrations of patience, understanding, kindness, and empathy, can help their children feel loved and accepted. They can help them feel a sense of belonging—being treasured and valued in the family.

Older children in this third plane begin to test their parents' patience, and it is important for parents to keep their composure and maintain an openness of understanding. At this point, parents should begin to embody an empathic stoicism and present themselves as a well of wisdom rather than of direct confrontation. This is key to instilling the value in treasuring and maintaining loving relationships as they transition through the planes of development. However, this stoicism can be a balancing act as parents still need to be actively involved in their children's social interests and help vet others to always ensure positive influences are entering their children's lives. This vetting process is both protective and instructive as the parent is creating templates of proper sets of values to enable children to recognize negative influencers and filter them out.

One of the most important lessons for children to learn in this stage is how family, the people we love and care about, can be protected from outside societal threats—family protects family. For children, a secure and protected home and a loving family who supports them are obviously important. However, children who also possess honed skills that they can contribute to the family and that the family appreciates will always make them feel like they belong and are not alone. We must understand that a child's identity is determined in part by the value he builds for himself, how he's recognized by his family, and his confidence in knowing the place he can call home. Without a place one can call home, without loving people who have one's back and can provide support, and without a skill to give oneself value, a person will struggle with not having an identity and will not know where they belong in society. Family is the only and the strongest bond that helps children in discovering their own identity and in searching for and maintaining successful, loving relationships.

## The Fourth Plane of Child Development, Age Eighteen to Twenty-Four

In the fourth plane of development, the child is now a young adult and is experiencing an explosion into the exploration of adult life, with all its challenges. They experience an emergence into young adulthood, trying to further figure out their place in society.[42] This is the bigger picture of society that now extends outside the family since there is now more interaction with the outside world via going to university, getting employment, or taking on a business.

The whole experience in this plane helps the young adult clarify their purpose and place in life and reach maturity. They will contemplate starting their own family. They will evolve into a morally, ethically, and socially responsible citizen. They will start to understand the importance of community and the levels of toxicity that exist and can pose a threat. Because of all the experiences and accomplishments of the previous years, the young adult will develop into a confident, competent learner, who is academically and emotionally prepared to succeed in whatever undertaking they may pursue, as well as being capable of sustaining healthy relationships. This is where we, as parents, understand that it wasn't all about the academics learned, but about the family values, the skills, and the knowledge necessary for our children to have a successful life finding happiness and fulfillment. All the decisions and choices made come down to the quality of adult that the child has become. This is why family values, virtues, culture, and traditions are far more important when it comes down to the legacy that is left behind with the future generations of the family tree. This is why it's important for us to secure those elements even in the previous developmental planes— those things that will help the next generation ensure the family legacy survives for many years into the uncertain future.

---

42   Ibid.

· · · ·

The knowledge of the planes of development allows parents to recognize, identify, and understand their children as they mature. They are then able to change and adjust how they engage to successfully meet their developmental needs. Learning is part of children's developmental needs, so how we educate children takes an important role in their healthy growth. Seizing the opportunities for making the most of the sensitive periods that children go through will make learning a lot easier and more natural. This is not only with regard to how children's intellect develops and evolves but also to how they develop into a complete person by becoming a confident and fulfilled adult ready to take on their future. There is no such thing as "falling behind" when a child is right where they need to be in their healthy development. This is not something that state schools can claim they provide as the students who have attended have shown one or more of the following: unpreparedness, lack of confidence, social awkwardness, and emotional instability. Another thing to note with respect to the planes of development is that any shifts of characteristics observed in children that do not line up with the planes of development just mean an early achievement of mastery or the lack thereof. It is something that knowledge and understanding of the planes can help parents gauge and, if necessary, make tweaks and adjustments to help correct/guide children onto their unique path of success.

We still hear anecdotes from public school teachers who claim that homeschooled children who return to the government system are "so far behind." These are misleading.

The simple explanation is that those particular teachers only have had contact with the few children who return to government schools—not the many who never do because their parents homeschooled *correctly*. And by *correctly*, we mean that the parents did *not* attempt to recreate the Prussian model at home. Instead, the learning felt natural to their children—like it was how it was always supposed to be. Those precious moments from the child's preschool years—which parents fondly recall as "the fun years"—don't end. Homeschooling simply extends them and prolongs them through the rest of childhood. Again, it's the parent-child bond that is the most important aspect of homeschooling.

# CHAPTER 5

# Deconstructing Curricula— Why the "Right" Curriculum Is Not as Important as You Think

A common impulse for a fledgling homeschool parent is to take to social media to ask about "the best homeschool curriculum." The response is a cacophony of confusing directions that overwhelms the already timid parent. If this was or is you, you are fortunate to be reading this book because we've got you covered. We'll offer you some relief in a moment.

First things first: let's get clear on what we mean by *curriculum*. When educators talk about curriculum, they are generally referring to the information and approach related to academics in which the subjects to be covered generally fall under language arts, mathematics, social studies, science, foreign languages, computer competency, art, music, health education, and physical education.

These curricula and their subjects came to be based on various academic institutions and private corporations writing and selling their wares under the auspices of creating "standards" to help students perform to academic excellence and achieve readiness for higher learning goals, providing high-quality academic standards for literacy and equipping students with the skills and knowledge necessary for success. However, there is nothing unique about standards that you should understand, other than they are, by design, minimum acceptable standards. It's comparable to the national electric code that electricians and electrical engineers must abide by, which represents the minimum safety standards to be applied to the designs so that the electrical systems installed don't catch on fire. Even though it's a safe approach to meet the minimum standards, it doesn't mean that the electrical systems installed work properly or even meet or exceed the expectations of the customer.

The bottom line is that the promise of academic excellence through the school's standards and curricula is no guarantee of high-quality learning or success. All the flowery language of the academics aside, for high-quality learning and success to happen, they must be custom made for the child. This tailored approach is the only guarantee that will work with your unique child in mind and will truly help them succeed in life.

After a few years of homeschooling, families quickly learn that the academic subjects are not as important as everything else the children are learning throughout their daily experiences. The parents realize that the academic subjects are not as difficult or time consuming for their children as the parents once remembered. Instead, the children then are enriching themselves with skills like cooking, sewing, gardening, and fixing broken items that are necessary for life. They are absorbing the culture, traditions, and values upheld in the family. They pick up on the social graces, courtesies, and communication demonstrated by the socially experienced adults in their environment. They learn healthy habits through practice and under the guidance of those who love them and have personal vested interest in their success. As opposed to being in an environment of structure and standardization, children are now in an environment that fosters imagination and creativity.

It's in this newly found freedom from stress and coercion that children can now discover their motivation to pursue what interests them and brings meaning to their lives. They can now live in the moment and be allowed to be curious and follow through with discovery. This is how children can get a rich imagination that helps them create new things. It is also this free imagination that will, in turn, inspire or motivate them to continue to want to learn and be creative.

Imagination cannot be taught from a curriculum. Not even creativity can be taught that way. Imagination and creativity are born within the self—in a low-stress environment of pursuing one's own agency. If you think you get creativity and imagination elsewhere, then it's merely copying and not the same. If the parents foster discovery and invention in the homeschool environment, then the children will develop their own imagination, and it's these opportunities that will help them become creative. This born creativity is what allows mankind to bring innovation to the world.

So *curriculum* in the traditional sense on its own cannot give children what they need in order to mature into capable problem solvers with practical skills as it's designed to merely disseminate information and not test or explore reason, logic, or analytical thinking. That doesn't mean, however, we should disregard curriculum entirely. We just need to define it, create it, and customize it.

You have an opportunity to savor one of the greatest benefits of home-based education—you get to custom tailor any and all curriculum to your child's needs. Not even the best, costliest, most acclaimed boxed curriculum can do this, however close to the mark it may be. What we're really doing at this point is demystifying and even redefining the word curriculum. Curriculum is just information—your body of resources. Your curriculum can be formal or informal, highly structured or merely a framework. You can even just use the term *information base* if you desire. It is the set of all information you will ever want to convey to your child. In other words, you are your own curriculum board.

That being said, is there any value in including the typical academic subjects in your child's information base? This is the question that every parent should be asking as the criteria to be applied against every subject the child needs or wants to learn. The questions, "Why do we learn anything, and for what purpose do we learn it?" are the questions that the parents need to answer and be able to translate to their children.

There is such a thing as an overwhelming amount of information that really is not necessary or valuable for certain goals in life. We all made it to adulthood, we know what it takes to succeed in life, we know what mistakes we made and learned from, and most importantly, we know what it takes to be a healthy and happy adult. Your experience is the first gauge to measure how much information was useful and valuable to your life; weigh that against how you would like your child's experience to be.

Homeschoolers quickly learn that not all information is necessary or valuable—and some information is downright harmful. Parents as protectors of their children should protect their children's minds. They need to distinguish between the information they think is absolutely necessary for their children to remember indefinitely and the information that just comes by as filler. Take any information on any subject and discriminate against it. Decide what would be good to know and trash the rest.

Children with their immature minds cannot handle an overwhelming amount of information and data. They quickly reach an overload, and their brains freeze. You will see children get bored, distracted by other things, or even shut down. This is a state in which learning does not happen, and even worse, it affects motivation. This is a state that children should not be in if they are expected to learn and, most importantly, to love the process of learning.

You can look at it from a business sense. Your homeschool is your business, and the children learning from it are your customers. You want them to be satisfied and happy. Use the observation skills from the three pillars—philosophy, methodology, observation—to gain information or perform a customer satisfaction survey to ask the children what they think about their homeschool. This feedback is a tool in itself in helping a parent decide what needs to be worked on in their homeschool to improve their customer satisfaction.

Any readily available curriculum that you can purchase is just a representation of information with a given approach to teaching it. Again, it's a standard that an individual came up with, without any input from the uniqueness of your child. Instead of accepting a standard of knowledge, parents need to look at information in a different way. Information about anything can be found in many different types of resources (textbooks, online videos, audiobooks, etc.).

In other words, the information on any subject found in any of the resources is your *information base*. It's anything that can be used by anyone to learn about or enjoy. A parent has the freedom to dissect/dismantle any resource, select the pieces to be used for learning, and discard the rest. A parent can tailor any *information base* to meet their child's needs and interests.

# Tailoring Teaching to Learning Styles: Auditory, Visual, Kinesthetic

There are three main types of learning styles: auditory, visual, and kinesthetic. Based on the child's learning style, pieces of information from certain resources can be selected to build your custom information base. This ensures that your child will have a successful reception of your information base. We will discuss each learning style so you can understand their differences.

In the **auditory learning style,** learners can easily process any information that they hear. Students in this category do well in the traditional classroom setting where a teacher provides the lectures, and the students who are good at processing information in this form are capable of successfully learning this way.

In the **visual learning style**, learners need visual stimulation in order to process the information being received. Students in this category sometimes do well in a traditional classroom setting where a teacher provides the lessons with the help of visual aids, and the students who are good at processing information in the form of pictures, charts, videos, maps, posters, drawings, et cetera are capable of learning successfully from this approach.

In the **kinesthetic learning style**, learners need to move in order to process the information being received. Students in this category do poorly in traditional classroom settings where a teacher forbids the students from any movement. A student who is good at processing information when some part of their body is moving will successfully learn in an environment where they have freedom of movement.

When selecting resources and pulling information from them, it is valuable to know what learning style the child does best with on any given subject. Some children will have a different learning style for every subject. Sometimes it's a combination of the learning styles. For example, a child can do well listening to an audiobook while manipulating learning materials with their hands. Another child may do better learning from a chart than reading the information directly from a book. If you understand your child's unique learning styles, you will be better equipped to develop a custom information base just for your child's learning needs.

## The Right Info at the Right Time: Beginner, Intermediate, and Advanced Curriculum

As we outlined in the section on mastery, there are different levels of expertise—beginner (familiarity), intermediate (proficiency), and advanced (mastery)—that a parent needs to consider when determining how much information is necessary or valuable for their children to know according to their plane of development. If parents start thinking that all they need to focus on is teaching beginner levels of expertise to their children when it comes to the academic subjects, then a lot of the intimidation and pressure will dissipate. Why do parents stress themselves so much, thinking that they are responsible for their children being at intermediate and advanced levels? Again, parents need to think about mastery in a different way. Just like for anyone, regardless of age, intermediate and /or advanced levels of expertise on any given subject or skill are best acquired out of free will.

When we homeschool, we are sending our children on a quest—a hero's journey. The parent is the quest-giver, but the hero faces the challenges. We parents have already passed our quests, and even if we don't remember how to defeat the final boss of algebra, we can guide the new hero—our child—to face their challenges. So don't worry if your history and English are a blur—they'll come back to you, and soon, you and your child will have leveled up together.

When children and parents decide to level up, that is a personal choice, and it is a commitment based on our own decisions to follow through and achieve, not forced upon us by someone else. If it's forced, then it's a struggle, and when it's a struggle, it's not enjoyable, which results in a failure. That could cause an emotional trauma that would be very challenging to overcome.

Instead of overcomplicating things and creating a wedge in the parent-child relationship or a block in the learning process, keep things simple at the beginner levels. Introductory lessons to concepts to give a superficial understanding is where the main focus should be. Parents will quickly get the feedback on whether these introductory lessons were fun and/or interesting because the children will naturally ask for more if they enjoyed it. That will dictate the pace on how the sequence is followed until you observe that the children have had their fill.

If a parent is not confident in the beginner levels, then that parent can assume the role of another classmate. For most children, learning alongside their parents is a special treat, so feel free to do this as another option. We recommend learning together with the children from time to time as it helps strengthen the parent-child bond. As a result, you will end up with many things in common, which makes the relationship much more meaningful.

Once the children have achieved mastery of beginner levels, then a parent can strategically leave easily accessible resources in the home for intermediate or advanced levels of expertise, and the children can decide to pursue further learning independently. This is usually in the planes of development in upper elementary–, middle school–, and high school–aged children. These children who have developed the agency and capability to learn independently naturally decide what they want to master at the higher levels of expertise.

Having conversations with older children is always necessary to gauge what their goals in life are. The children will tell their parents if they need their help in meeting those goals. Sometimes there's an additional resource you need to find, and that may be another adult who is an expert in that knowledge or skill. Apprenticeships or special tutelage may be required if a parent does not think they are qualified to teach at that advanced expert level.

Engage and have conversations with your children frequently, and you will find out what they need, what they want, and where they want to go in life.

## Concrete versus Abstract Information

The two most basic approaches to teaching are concrete and abstract teaching. The concrete approach uses concrete materials, also called manipulatives, for hands-on learning. Even advanced concepts can be easily learned when a sequence of introductory lessons given in concrete form is provided. Young children in the earlier planes of development naturally gravitate to the hands-on learning approach as they are curious about everything and want to learn about how and why things work. As a matter of fact, the concrete approach works well at any age—even in the later planes of development—because when a person learns something new at beginner levels, it is necessary to practice with the practical application of what's being learned to be able to grasp that level of competency.

The abstract approach works well when a higher level of competency already exists. In other words, a person is able to learn further by just imagining in their mind what is being explained without the need of the practical application. Usually, the abstract approach is used at advanced and sometimes intermediate levels. The right time to learn the abstract representation of a concept is after mastering the concrete representation of that same concept. There is a transition that happens from concrete to abstraction. The planes of development are your guide for this transition. As in the first half of each plane, the concrete aspect can be mastered, and in the second half of each plane, the abstract aspect can be introduced.

A perfect example of how this is used is in learning mathematics. We begin by learning the concept of numbers. If the first lessons go straight to writing numbers on paper, that is an abstract approach. Numbers on a piece of paper have no meaning to a child's developing mind. Rather than presenting that, the correct approach is to introduce concrete materials like blocks. The child can touch a block, and it represents one block. That now has meaning as they can touch what one means, and that's how the concept of one is learned. You can now bring in ten identical blocks, and the concept that they can be counted from one to ten can be presented. Soon, the child will master counting from one to ten and will be ready to learn that there is a way to represent the numbers that were counted concretely by writing them down on paper so that they can now be read. Once the child masters writing and reading numbers one to ten, the passage from concrete to abstraction for counting one to ten will be complete. After that, other mathematical concepts with similar concrete-to-abstract mathematical patterns can be mastered in the same way.

Parents must observe their children in order to know when they are ready for that passage to abstraction as a premature exposure to abstract information will not allow them to fully grasp the concepts. There is no point in learning anything unless it is learned well, even if it's at the beginner level. It's OK to have beginner skills in cooking and sewing, for example. Not everyone is going to want to become a chef or a seamstress, but it is useful to know enough for your own needs. It is the same with the academic subjects. Not everyone is going to want to become a mathematician or a scientist. Understand your children and help guide them to the joy of learning instead.

## The True Cost of Curriculum

Does it cost a fortune to develop the custom information base for your children? Not really. Books and other resources can be borrowed from the library at no cost. Concrete materials can be made at home at very little cost. There's a myriad of free resources online including those on how to make your own DIY learning materials and videos that show you how to learn anything. We'll share with you a list of our favorites in the next chapter.

The point is, your child's information base doesn't have to cost much, but it does require being open minded and creative. That time and effort used in creating a custom information base for your child is worth it because being in full control of what gets instilled in your children's minds is priceless.

# Boxed or Not Boxed?

If you need a turn-key, commercially available (boxed) curriculum to get you started homeschooling, I'm not going to disparage you. Just like going to the gym for the first time, just start. It gets easier and more challenging. Pretty soon, you are helping your neighbor begin homeschooling their children. There are plenty of boxed homeschooling curricula on the market—a lot more than thirty years ago—but however good they may be, they're still not tailored to your child or to your particular family values. They may be superior in many aspects to government schools, but only you can ensure that a connection between your children's unique learning style and the lessons to be conveyed exists.

There will also be moments when you begin homeschooling, and your child learns for the first time something outside the scope of that expensive homeschool curriculum you purchased. Or you find something in the curriculum that you would rather de-emphasize or go in a different direction with. In that moment, that pricey curriculum loses some value under a newfound personal sense of freedom and confidence. You may also realize that it's not choosing the right curriculum that is key—it's the health of the relationship between the parent and child. It is common that the more experience a parent gets, the less reliant they become on didactically following a curriculum, and the more it becomes merely a guide. This explains why some parents will still have problems with purchased curricula—they are trying to force the curriculum to work without reading the child. This affects the parent-child bond—the parent may still see some progress, but it's not optimal. However, with a healthy relationship, just about any curriculum will work—this is the strength and necessity of improving your relationship with your children. Remember to use the pillar of observation and watch for indicators of your methodology not working, then readjust back into alignment with your philosophy.

The perfect example of this is when a boxed curriculum comes with books to be used for reading and you notice that your child is not in the least bit interested in reading those particular books and hence is starting to miss out on learning to read. A conflict arises where your child doesn't want to read those books period. This means that the curriculum is not working out for your child. You need to think back to your philosophy of education on how children learn best and specifically on how your child learns best. As a result you recall that children need to enjoy the learning process and that children want to practice independence and agency. You adjust the methodology to now get other resources, like books from the library and this time allow your child to choose the books he would rather read from. You basically strayed away from that boxed curriculum and adopted a custom approach that better met your child's emergent needs. Now he has no problem with the learning process and happily reads his chosen books.

## Curriculum as Information: A Quick Recap

We hope by this point that the word *curriculum* is less scary than it may have felt in the past. It's an academic term, which is why we've reframed it as simply *information*. In our household, we've reframed the concept of *chores* as *skills* because it is far more appealing and descriptive to *build* skills than it is to *do* chores. Similar reframes work with other aspects of parenting, and home education is no exception.

We've covered a lot of ground in this chapter so far, so let's review the essential points:

- Curriculum is just information.
- Curriculum is *your* information—the lessons and values that you deem important.
- You can get information anywhere and everywhere.
- It is the information you want to share with your children.
- You don't need a boxed curriculum unless you want one.
- You can change it up to suit your needs.
- The curriculum must not degrade the parent-child bond.

Like we said, if you need a boxed curriculum to get you started homeschooling, that's OK. It is also OK if you complete your child's education by only using that purchased curriculum—especially if the curriculum is a good match for your child's needs. However, if there is to be a central principle or doctrine of homeschooling, it would be homeschooling is freedom.

You are free to use or not use resources—to use boxed or customized materials or to just wing it. The important thing is that you decide. Don't be discouraged if you are having trouble—just maintain that parent-child bond, and success will happen.

"But where do I find resources? What constitutes a resource?" We get these questions all the time, and the first thing we find is that many people haven't even done a basic internet search. If they did anything, it was to ask on social media—don't do this.

The resources to make homeschooling practical and affordable are everywhere, and they are very much accessible. Curriculum is one small aspect of it. The ideal time to begin thinking about homeschooling in general is right after the child is born. If homeschooling is parenting, the "school years" begin when the child is born, but they never end. There is no summer break from education for children, just as there is no "break" or pause in learning in real life.

The real reason to break free from the boundaries of curriculum is so children can learn anything they want or need to at their current plane of development and at their own pace. "Homeschooling" doesn't need to be your children sitting at the kitchen table with you providing direct instruction, forcing them through a boxed curriculum for a six- to eight-hour school day.

Now that we've established that the curriculum is for the children, and the children are not for the curriculum, we can break free from those restrictions. We can choose resources to help our children advance to mastery based on their learning styles. We even have the freedom to try various homeschooling techniques that may keep them engaged and interested on their way to independent learning. Homeschooling is all the resources you can use, all you get to choose, and all fully customizable.

# CHAPTER 6

# Can We Afford to Homeschool?

Did you know that the national average for the cost of homeschooling is just $600.00 per student, per year?[43] But just knowing that is not going to help you budget the adjustments you are going to make or have just made. We hear all the common excuses, "Well, homeschooling is great for those who can afford it" or "What about the poor? How are they going to homeschool?" or, "It takes two incomes just to make it!" There are many renditions of these dismissals and I'm sure you have heard many more examples, but the question is not answered by some one-size-fits-all style, central planning type solution—it's about your own family. What can *you* do to make homeschooling happen for *you*?

We don't claim to have the answers to every scenario on personal finance, but we can, and have, helped families discover new ways to think about their specific finances so they can meet their desire for a better life for their children. One general truth about human nature is that if we have a goal and a vision, we will do everything we can to make it happen. Let's dig into this.

Both of us, Jonathan and Adriana, as engineers, have presided over and contributed to massive engineering budgets over some of the largest projects

---

43  Ray, Brian D. "Research Facts on Homeschooling. National Home Education Research Institute." NHERI, May 11, 2023. https://www.google.com/url?q=https://www.nheri.org/research-facts-on-homeschooling/&sa=D&source=docs&ust=1682011936607931&usg=AOvVaw3OBotDxnkrjrqMySw4qyV3.

in the world. We have used many different tools to arrange tasks and milestones to manage budgetary constraints and cash flow. Of course we were part of a larger team of people from many different departments, but you get the idea that the understanding of complex systems helps to shed light on systems—even as small as family finances. It's this engineering ability to analyze systems, solve problems and provide solutions that is the key to what we do. We can suggest innovative new methods, provide guidance and present a simple plan for your family to begin that homeschooling venture.

That being said, the first thing you need is to firmly decide that you want to make homeschooling happen—to commit to the plan. So do this, write down your mission statement with your goals. This will help you keep your focus. A mission statement is a summary of your aims, goals, purpose, and values of your particular endeavor. Be as specific as you can like, "To create a homeschool that helps my children grow in knowledge and wisdom in a peaceful setting" and "Where I, the mother, can homeschool as a stay-at-home-mom and my husband works." You can even write a statement that includes, "Our vision that we will both be work-at-home parents to become more available to our children."

# Stop the Guessing and Start Knowing—Free Your Mind

The next thing to do is to free your mind from defeatist thinking such as thinking that homeschooling is an expense—it is not. Homeschooling is a multigenerational investment—as important as savings, retirement accounts, life insurance, 401k, etc. Except, you are banking on the vitality of your children's minds and the health of your family's relationships. The returns of this investment goes way beyond your children just acquiring knowledge - it's all the secondary benefits as well such as your children having better bonds with family, more freedom and creativity, healthy relationships with others, and making better life choices.

"But if we homeschool, one of us will have to quit - we can't afford to lose that income!" Ok, but how much will you save by not working?

Here are some common expenses that are freed up by a wife *not having* a typical office job:

- Gasoline
- Mileage, car wear & tear (IRS $0.65/mile)
- Tolls, parking, tickets
- Car washes
- Additional car payments
- Lunches and dinners out
- Dry cleaning
- Wardrobe, shoes, outfits
- Makeup and accessories
- Spa, salon, and health treatments
- Gym memberships
- Childcare/daycare

All of these inputs can now be calculated in a Cost-Benefit Analysis (a comparison between costs and benefits of a proposal) to provide a clear picture of the proposal. We might even consider the husband homeschooling and the wife working. However, we recommend this with older children only. We even know a homeschooling family who both work and the three children do their lessons on the weekends.

"But I'm a single parent!" We know, we get it. Some of our clients are single parents also and they struggle with a lot of issues not related to homeschooling. However, it may take some time for you (and many others) to realize their resolve to homeschool their children. As we have said, we may not address here the time and financial solutions to your particular scenario, but we do provide one-on-one coaching to show different ways to think about your own personal situation. The best thing to keep in mind is, whatever situation you are in, you can put in the effort to make it better. Let's now examine some practical avenues for saving money on tools and resources.

# Free (or Nearly Free) Homeschool Resources

As a general rule, never pay full price for books if you can help it—in fact, it doesn't have to be just about books either! Try to get discounts and freebies everywhere. Some places even extend teacher discounts to homeschoolers—just ask them. But remember that you can find deals everywhere. Here is a list of the most common free (or nearly free) resources for homeschoolers:

- The library (books, magazines, videos, audiobooks, events, computer labs)
- YouTube (DIY, lessons, guides)
- Internet (Free resources such as printable activities, maps, charts)
- Free online academies, courses, and classes (e.g., Khan Academy)
- Used bookstores (old textbooks are great—a lot of times better than new)
- Office supply stores (supplies and materials—check the bargain bin)
- Garage sales (especially garage sales from former homeschoolers)
- Public school dumpsters (yes, this is a thing! Schools throw out a lot of stuff)
- Dollar stores/General stores (look for the discounted items after the school rush)
- Other homeschoolers (e.g., curriculum swapping, co-ops)
- Outings and field trips (e.g., museums, planetariums)
- Your own backyard or neighborhood park (opportunities for lessons or gathering specimens)
- Your own knowledge and experiences (a lot of you have a wealth of life experience—talk to grandma and grandpa!)

You don't have to spend a dollar to homeschool your children for them to reach mastery and become independent self-learners. We've found that when parents are concerned about the cost of curriculum, co-ops, field trips, and other expenses that can add up, there is usually a different hidden concern they're less likely to reveal right away, such as a reluctance to make changes to other aspects of their lives: e.g., luxury and/or entertainment expenses for the adults.

# You Can Make it Happen

To recap, we've reviewed many low and no-cost options for many children's information bases, so it's established that homeschooling can be done for free or nearly free. As we have pointed out, the national average for homeschooling expenditure is only $600 per child per year. It is usually true that when parents bring up financial considerations of homeschooling, they're talking about the loss of employment income—not the actual cost of coursework and textbooks. The pervasive belief among non-homeschoolers is that this is "too expensive" or "too disruptive." They believe one parent would have to quit their full-time job.

When we've had exchanges with parents who bring up these excuses, that's all they are—excuses. Neither parent *has* to quit their job. Lessons can be completed on a couple of evenings a week and one or two days on the weekend, all the while the children are learning independently and continuing on with their love of learning. Several Homeschool Life community members are working parents; Mom and Dad both have full-time jobs. There are even full-time-working single parents. What you perceive as difficult about homeschooling becomes easy when you've decided to make it work—when you've *decided* that the benefits far outweigh the costs. Then the excuses are gone and you realize that you can make it happen.

We understand that your family may not be able to transition to homeschooling immediately, but you can prepare to homeschool in 3, 6, or even 9 months. Your family may need to switch jobs, get a side hustle or multiple side hustles, enlist the help of grandparents, or any one of hundreds of solutions. The fact is, if you want to change the path your family is on, you have that power, and if you need help or even to bounce off ideas, you can contact Homeschool Life and schedule a coaching session—we'd love to talk to you.

# CHAPTER 7

# The Ten Most Common Homeschooling Styles

Not all homeschooling is the same. You have the information you want to share with your children; now what methodology or approach do you want to use to share it? There are numerous styles of home-based education. Just as in painting, there are many styles such as impressionism, expressionism, abstract, or surrealism; each style has its own technique.

In other words, your approach or technique with any of these styles may vary but still be categorized within a particular style. Below is a list of some of the most common styles of homeschooling that you may encounter, with a brief description of each. All of them have rich histories and explanations that are too long to do justice to in this book alone, so we encourage you to explore them further. Each is centered around a main goal and promotes a particular approach to educating children. Sometimes a decision made on a particular style is based on meeting a particular family need, and sometimes it is based on convenience. Some are secular, and some are religion based. Some focus on the study of academic subjects, and others do not. Some require a specific curriculum to be used and others are more flexible.

Here are the ten.

# Classical Homeschooling

*Classical* refers to the centuries-old Greek methodology used in the Middle Ages through the Renaissance called the *trivium* (the grammars, logic, and rhetoric). The premise is that students learn facts and data in grammar school (elementary), logic and critical thinking in middle school, and rhetoric and self-expression in high school. Classical education has structured, full days and follows a reading plan.

Classical education often incorporates the learning of Greek and Latin. Reading is a high priority as students are expected to become familiar with key texts across the history of Western civilization. Classical schooling also features the use of Socratic dialogue to foster discussion and debate. This reinforces logic as critical thinking from classical Aristotelian logic or as lateral thinking and problem-solving. In practice, many classical homeschoolers place a heavy emphasis on Bible study and biblical worldview training.

The classical education's limitation is that it is not practical for most families; it can place a lot of pressure on children who are not good at or interested in heavy reading or rigorous, structured schedules. Classical education does not provide clear avenues for practicing and developing agency because of its authoritarian nature. It also doesn't provide the hands-on learning, experimentation, and discovery that children need to develop creativity. It is more applicable for the older child who is ready to transition to the abstract.

# Classical Conversations

This style was created in the late 1990s for parents who want Christian- and family-friendly home education. It focuses on three things: the classics, Christianity, and community. Classical and religious elements are instilled in the academic curriculum choices.

Classical conversations are community based, so families are never alone on the homeschool journey. A core tenet is for a homeschooling family to join other families within the classical conversations co-op.

Its limitation is that it does not provide the flexibility and freedom to teach and/or learn differently, and the child is not presented opportunities to be a self-learner. There also may not be a co-op in your area. Parents are expected to purchase the curriculum and follow it as instructed, be part of the co-op, and volunteer time for community participation.

## Charlotte Mason

This homeschooling style was developed by British educator Charlotte Mason, a nineteenth-century homeschooling pioneer. It incorporates short, structured lessons, typically in the mornings. Afternoons are spent outdoors enjoying nature, usually via nature walks and journaling. Touting a three-pronged philosophy of education—discipline (good habits), life ("living" academics), and atmosphere (a child's surroundings)—Charlotte Mason also focuses on practice in observation, memorization, and narration.

The appeal to some families is the application of religion to their daily studies, especially with regular scripture memorization. The curriculum also involves reading "living books," which are stories written by someone who has experienced the subject firsthand and teaches those learned life lessons.

Its limitation is that it was originally designed in the nineteenth century for the elementary child. Since then, others have adapted it to the higher grades, so one can expect some philosophical divergence from Ms. Mason's own writings and intentions toward other education models. In middle school and high school, the Charlotte Mason curriculum begins to resemble traditional academics.

# Waldorf Homeschool

The Waldorf School was developed by Rudolf Steiner in the early 1900s as a holistic approach to education. It wasn't initially developed as a homeschool style but as a private school with an emphasis on the whole child (head, heart, and hands) while focusing heavily on the arts, folklore, mythology, and the natural world.

Steiner's pedagogical approach used the proto-psychological, Greco-Roman concept of the four humors—melancholic, sanguine, phlegmatic, and choleric—in defining the learning styles of children. At lower levels, rhythm and consistency are important, so the design of the daily schedule is to flow easily, allowing parents time to manage responsibilities. At higher levels, autonomous learning is encouraged.

The main appeal for families is the combination of the arts with the academics. Most families who come from the fine arts industry like musicians, artists, and performers may find this to be a good fit.

Its limitation, though, is that it has a heavy emphasis on the arts and may not be a good fit for some children whose talents lie elsewhere. It may also be difficult academically to prepare children for higher learning. Some Waldorf curriculum builders have recently become more politically left leaning in their agendas, which may not coincide with some parents' values.

# Unschooling

Unschooling was developed by John Holt, a homeschooling pioneer in the 1950s. His revolutionary approach was based on the premise that children are more likely to fail at learning when taught in the compliance-based public (Prussian) school system—mainly because children learn best when they are not pressured to learn in a way that is of no interest to them. Holt theorized that children are more motivated to learn when they do it in their own way and on their own terms. Parents are then more of a resource to provide the information at the request of their children.

Unschooling "curriculum" varies from home to home, is often planned the same day, and is child led. In some homes, the learning is entirely up to the children; in other homes, the learning is a balance between what the children want to learn and what the parents want to present as learning material. The appeal of this style is the flexibility of not having to resemble learning in the school system. It is popular and effective for parents with children whose learning style and personality are such that the traditional school system seems tedious, boring, and slow paced and who want something that could rekindle the joy of learning so that they can display their prowess.

Unschooling's biggest concern and limitation is that, for many parents, the "child-leading" element is not well understood, and they fail in its application. This causes the child to miss being exposed to enough learning materials. If they are considering higher learning, they will find themselves unprepared for a future in academia as a result of being unschooled.

# Montessori

Montessori-style education did not start out as a homeschooling system but was developed by Dr. Maria Montessori in the late 1890s as an alternative to the traditional school system. From her research, she discovered that the way children learn is very different from the traditional school system. In Montessori, children have full agency on what they are learning and learn in a prepared environment.

This methodology was created to satisfy the classroom setting for students to learn in by making the classroom resemble the comforts and feel of a home. Children share the classroom with other age groups (a three-year range) to resemble a community where children are younger or older by a few years. Instead of toys, the children have access to specially designed hands-on materials, also called "work" or "manipulatives." These manipulatives were specifically designed not only to appeal to the children but also to help develop fine or gross motor skills and to help students grasp basic concepts that build on other concepts in preparation for more advanced ideas. The dynamics of children freely choosing these activities, watching others use them, and being introduced to new ones are the application of Dr.

Montessori's philosophy of allowing children to discover, or, as she says, "Let the child lead." This premise carries over to the homeschool version of the Montessori method. Dr. Montessori's research on the stages of development in children and on how children learn is what caused her to create the planes of development. It's through the understanding of the planes of development that any person would begin to understand how the environment children are in and the materials they are exposed to can influence them and satisfy (or not) their developmental needs.

In the homeschool Montessori application, there is opportunity for the children to learn to manage their own time. There are readily available learning materials that promote experimentation and discovery. As per Dr. Montessori's philosophy, the concept of the prepared environment is key—each environment (and the manipulatives) evolves with the child as the child transitions through the planes of development. This environment allows children to feel safe and secure. They are surrounded by beauty and interesting materials, which lead them to imagination and creativity. There is also a clear delineation and passage between the concrete and abstract. The Montessori materials can be purchased, they can be made (DIY), or others can be chosen or created as long as they meet the philosophy behind Montessori.

Montessori's appeal to some families is how thorough and well established this method is. It's backed by neuroscience as an effective way to learn naturally and develop strong skills in and understanding of anything, including the academic subjects. Parents are in full control of what resources and materials to bring into the prepared environment. It is very flexible in the sense that the best elements found in the other homeschool styles can easily be incorporated within the choices of resources and activities made available to the children.

Children develop high agency and become independent in their learning. They also gain a love for learning, which makes the achievement of higher learning effortless. Families who are forward thinking and open to innovation appreciate the elegance of this method.

As successful as Montessori is, it has its limitations. Parents need to have a strong understanding of the philosophy as it is a much different approach than what they are used to. Some families might feel intimidated by having to put time and effort into grasping the foundation in order to gain its benefits. Some families may feel that they must purchase the expensive Montessori learning materials—even without understanding their purpose. Worse, they might think that the materials are just toys to be played with. Some parents may feel challenged by the responsibility of developing unique lessons and materials for their children. Some may even be discouraged when they realize the amount of personal study and reading that is required to fully understand the philosophy and apply it correctly.

# School at Home

School at home should not be considered homeschooling. It just brings the public school into your house. It is structured and uses a state-approved (or accepted) packaged curriculum that is all planned out. Sometimes the plan is fully computer based. Other times, it is an online program sponsored by the local public school system.

The appeal to some families is its convenience and the fact that it meets the standards of the law. Some parents who are not confident may find the other homeschooling styles too challenging and, hence, stressful to pursue and so choose this path of least resistance for themselves as the role of the parent is reduced to an overseer rather than a teacher. Its limitation, though, is that it is inflexible and does not allow children the freedom to discover and be creative. It doesn't take into account the uniqueness of the child or their strengths or weaknesses, nor does it incorporate the personal interests the child may have. Some children may experience conflict with its restrictions and may lose motivation to want to learn further on their own.

# Unit Studies

Unit studies are touted as an integrated approach to learning in which a central theme is chosen, and all possible connections to that theme are explored in each lesson. This is also known as thematic instruction and is related to interdisciplinary or phenomenon-based learning. Unit studies can be captivating to students who have a natural desire to know everything about a topic. In other words, it focuses on incorporating mathematics, English language, social studies, art, and anything else that can be linked to the theme chosen.

The appeal to some families is it seems like it would be creative and perhaps fun to exhaust every subtopic of a given theme. Its limitation, though, is that the children are not the ones making the connections and having those aha self-discovery moments for themselves as all is revealed to them by the parents. There could also be some learning gaps where the children may not be ready to fully comprehend certain concepts to make the proper connections and understand the intended meaning behind them. The academic subjects usually have their own logic and sequence and hence do not work well when all are tied to the same theme. This may end with the child stuck in inner conflict and confusion. The children do not get a solid understanding of the true bigger picture because there is no unified set of ideas to bring it all together. In practice, boredom and the sense of "being lectured to" are common reports on this style.

# Eclectic/Relaxed Homeschooling

The eclectic/relaxed homeschool style brings flexibility to the point where families have no particular loyalty to any one curriculum or style but exercise the freedom to pick and choose as needs arise. Mornings are often used for more formal work, and afternoons are used for hobbies and other special projects. There are no specific times set, but the child is expected to meet certain educational goals. The appeal to some families is that it's flexible and allows them to be open to trying new things. Its limitation is that it may leave indecisive parents unable to choose wisely. Sometimes, these homeschools can be too hasty in discarding good methodology that some other styles bring to the table. By not investing the time in understanding them fully, they lose the opportunity to gain those benefits.

# Forest School

Forest school was created in the 1950s in two different countries, Denmark and Sweden. It is an outdoor education in which students spend time in natural environments to learn personal, social, and technical skills. It is described as an inspirational process through which children feel motivated and engaged while at the same time developing a deeper connection with nature. There are opportunities for some hands-on learning, which develops their confidence. The appeal to some families is that it presents as a good fit for children who would benefit from exploring the outside world and learning some great skills. Its limitation is that it doesn't cover the academic subjects, so those children who want to pursue higher learning would not be prepared for that future.

. . . .

This list of homeschooling styles is neither authoritative nor exhaustive. Please don't feel like you must tie your family to a particular style. Borrow from whichever resonates with you at this time or in a future season of your child's learning. Just like with curriculum, where you're pulling greatly from one, perhaps you pick and choose different homeschooling approaches as needed. Perhaps you unschool in the summer, use computer-based learning during the day, and work in some forest schooling on the weekends. Focus on what's best for your child and what you're capable of. You don't have to choose one (or all) of them, and there's no reason for guilt if you feel you're unable for whatever reason to try Montessori or any other system. Find or develop a system that works because homeschooling is what you and your family want and need it to be.

Feel free to gravitate toward however many you need, and don't be fixated on or stuck with any one of them. Continue to explore more at your convenience. The fastest and cheapest way to research any of these methods is to search for free introductory videos online. Look up examples as well so you can see other children experiencing that approach to homeschool. Can you imagine your child working well with unit studies, for example? If so, then try it, and if it works out, keep at it. If not, that's OK. There's more to research and test to see what works with your family.

We're not telling you what curriculum to use, and for some, that may be the hardest sticking point in homeschooling. So often, parents new to homeschooling or at least considering it visit homeschooling groups in person or join a forum online, and their first post is along the lines of "What curriculum should I use?" Only your children can teach you what they want to learn; no other parent can tell you. We can offer you options and suggest how to begin learning more about whichever approaches may resonate with your children. But only you can decide on your own and for yourself what you and your children are emotionally ready to try in any of these approaches.

Remember, this is not the homeschooling of the 1980s, filled with headbanded, Birkenstock-wearing, wheat germ–munching, commune hippies teaching barefooted children named Skye and Freedom from worn-out college textbooks. We have evolved; we have tech resources at our fingertips. We create online content and connect with people in other countries. We can move and adjust at the speed of the internet and coordinate outings and field trips with our whole community by simply posting to our Facebook groups. That being said, our radical approach to homeschooling should be revealing itself to you by now. Just wait. There's more to this approach—and much more to unlearn from the old paradigms.

# CHAPTER 8

# How Much Time to Actually Spend Homeschooling

"How long should we actually homeschool our kids?" We hear this daily. The parents aren't asking about years or grades. They mean hours in the day. And usually when they ask, it's because they hold an unspoken fear of failing to meet the expectations of the law. Or perhaps they worry their child will fall behind their local educational standards. In many US states, homeschooling laws require academic subjects to be covered in the same way the homeschooled children would learn were they in school. These academic subjects include mathematics, science, social studies, language arts (English, in the US), foreign language, health and fitness, art and music. All these are generally covered in institutions on an annual basis, from elementary through high school, and it takes, on average, 6.5 hours, five days a week to do so (the standard school day).

We all know by now that the Prussian system–based school is very different from home-based education. Most of the time spent (wasted) in school institutions is spent managing large numbers of students, and only a fraction of the time is invested in actual teaching or learning of the aforementioned academic subjects. But in the homeschool setting, a one-on-one approach is almost infinitely more efficient and meaningful to each and every child.

When thinking about the time needed to homeschool your children, compare the inefficient Prussian model to the home-based education option, in which students actually enjoy learning and are more apt to remember the information indefinitely and, hence, master it. The ultimate test of whether a subject is mastered or not is whether the learner can, in turn, teach it to others. In other words, has the student become the instructor?

We realize that homeschooling parents just want to know how long their days should be, and we'll get to specific numbers and even academic subject schedule examples shortly. But again, understand that many parents confuse time spent teaching each academic subject every day with actual *learning*. The school system on which this is based, however, is woefully inefficient compared to homeschool. Any subject or skill can be learned in a fraction of the time because of the home educator's one-on-one format, the stress-free environment at home, and the fact that the child is more likely to be thinking creatively in their learning.

That being said, the old ways die hard. A common mistake we see some homeschool parents make is trying to take advantage of efficiency to pack even more academic training into less time every day. All soon discover through bitter conflict that children have their own limitations. These must not be ignored if you want the homeschool experience to be a positive and successful one. Children, depending on their age, maturity, and learning ability, have varying attention spans. Children are also only able to focus on a given academic subject for a particular, limited length of time. Parents must use their observation skills to gauge when the children have "had enough" of any particular subject. Perhaps the child is bored, tired, just no longer interested, or unable to have fun with it.

# "You Mean I Don't Have to Spend Hours and Hours Homeschooling?"

To understand the importance of implementing the correct learning environment in the homeschool, we need to understand what attention is. Attention is also called concentration. It is a cognitive development skill that acts as an executive function controlled by the frontal lobe of the brain. Attention is a process when in an environment filled with stimuli, information is first detected, and the information that is considered useful is selected, hence sustained. Research has shown that it follows a relatively straightforward predetermined trajectory. This means that as the brain develops and matures, the attention span will increase. Attention also plays an important role in the development of other areas like short-term memory, long-term memory, comprehension, sensory skills, language, and more. Other research has determined that attention and memory affect learning and predict its effects on future academic achievement. In other words, the better the attention skills developed early on, the more success the child will have in continuing to learn, and they will be more apt to succeed in academics in the future.[44]

Attention can also be affected by technology. In our current fast-paced modern world, it is now common for children to be bombarded with technology of every kind (television, smartphones, computers, tablets, smart watches, etc.). Technology has some negative impacts on attention, one of them being overstimulation. It's difficult to compete with other methods of learning useful information like wooden educational toys or books when tablet computers or video games are present. Preference for technology narrows down learning method choices. The overstimulation also causes dopamine hits to the brain because of the instant gratification received from all the thrills and dynamics that keep children enthralled, which can result in developing an addiction that, in turn, can cause other problems like behavioral and health issues. There is a better way to introduce technology—as a tool for learning rather than for entertainment—that will be discussed

---

44  Dr. Lisa G. Hahn, "How Long Can Your Child Pay Attention?" Morris Psychological Group, November 10, 2020, https://morrispsych.com/how-long-can-your-child-pay-attention-by-dr-lisa-g-hahn-ph-d-abbp/.

later on. The truth of the matter is that for a developing brain, little to no technology is best for developing attention skills and, thus, learning. Knowing that, here is a starting point for matching a child's education at different ages to their corresponding attention span.[45]

There are minimum and maximum amounts of time per day a child is capable of learning a concept, subject, or skill. We also note when breaks are needed and where ceasing study altogether for the day is necessary. The one exception is those instances when the child is genuinely interested in that subject or skill and is therefore capable of exceeding the amount of time estimated. This is decided by their own sense of agency.

### SUSTAINED ATTENTION BY GRADE

| Grade Level | Minimum | Maximum | Recommended Length Sustained Attention |
|---|---|---|---|
| PreK | 20 minutes/day | 60 minutes/day | 3-5 minutes |
| K | 30 minutes/day | 90 minutes/day | 3-5 minutes |
| 1-2 | 45 minutes/day | 90 minutes/day | 5-10 minutes |
| 3-5 | 60 minutes/day | 120 minutes/day | 10-15 minutes |
| 6-8 | Class: 15 minutes/day<br>Total: 90 minutes/day | Class: 30 minutes/day<br>Class: 180 minutes/day | 1 subject area or class |
| 9-12 | Class: 20 minutes/day<br>Total: 120 minutes/day | Class: 45 minutes/day<br>Class: 270 minutes/day | 1 subject area or class |

This chart was inspired by the National Board for Professional Teaching Standards and was originally published by the Illinois State Board of Education, the South Carolina Department of Education, and other state boards during the pandemic. This was their desperate attempt to help parents with doing public school at home with their children. The irony, of course, is that it reveals what children are actually capable of sustaining at their age—and how much more efficient learning at home is compared to the wasted hours during which children are kept in institutions every day. It has been made obvious that schools are glorified babysitting services for working parents. Any learning that happens is minimal. And again, the quality is woefully inferior to homeschooling.[46]

---

45  Ibid
46  Ibid.

Academics in general exist to help children develop and achieve the logical and organized thinking necessary for the higher learning levels. By studying academics (such as math, science, English, etc.), children are expected to obtain problem-solving skills, analytical abilities, effective communication, creativity, and innovation. However, the traditional school system with its high expectations ignores some of the most basic pedagogical knowledge to elevate students to these levels. Instead of building a strong academic base with concrete materials and then introducing abstract representation over time, it uses the abstract to try to explain the concrete—a familiar observation in the failed Common Core curriculum.

As with all child development insights and homeschooling tips, the most practical approach is to assess your own children. Provide them with time and flexibility that takes into account their unique strengths and challenges. Allow them to practice honing their attention skills so learning becomes easier, and mastery becomes possible.

Consider the homeschool day from the highest-level perspective. Just because younger children have a relatively short attention span for academic study does not mean they are relegated to learning only during those hours. What makes homeschooling unique, effective, and efficient is that the world is your classroom, society offers classmates, and learning happens 24-7 and all year round. There are no set boundaries or restrictions on when children can learn. They absorb all the information in their surroundings and constantly engage with society. Learning is a part of life. It's not something you have to schedule or force children to sit still at a desk to experience. Again, homeschool is not meant to be a replica of a restricted environment, one not of children's own choosing, where they're forced to retain mostly useless or meaningless information and where they're made to learn according to only one particular approach. The school system in all its glory can be suffocating for children who have the potential to excel greatly in their own way.

As we've made clear already, we are not throwing the academic baby out with the Prussian system's bath water. In Homeschool Life, we help families who want to teach academic subjects do just that. How? you might wonder. Well, assessing the children, understanding how each child uniquely learns, and then discovering what they're passionate about—all these come first, prior to any academic training. Each and every family's homeschool—with the children's input—determines the duration of what is covered.

Let's say a family wants to cover pre-algebra. Depending on the child's interest and ability and the resource used (textbook or computer based), they would discuss together as a family how much time to invest. For some kids, pre-algebra can be studied to the point of mastery in six months. Others might take a year and a half or longer.

The duration also depends on how much time the child wants to spend weekly or biweekly to cover a certain number of chapters and complete the exercises in a book. Often at the pre-algebra age, most children are entirely independent learners and can accomplish this on their own. Others may need interaction with parents to develop competence. This is where the tailoring of information happens when it comes to academics. The more flexible you make the subject's study, the easier it is for students to set a comfortable pace at which they can learn and master a subject.

We brought up independent learning a few times in the previous chapters. Understand that many homeschool families have children who are highly motivated to pursue their own interests. Parents need to simply let them pursue those interests without fretting over academic study. Often, the children's interests fall under specific academic subjects. At other times, they're useful, necessary skills. The challenge is really for the parents, who must capture these efforts and record progress as education credits. (Chapter 10 covers this.) All learning and the acquisition of mastery is education. Since learning happens at all times (including evenings, weekends, and holidays), and homeschooling looks very different from the institutions, it still should be noted as proof that learning is happening and that the homeschooling law is indeed being met.

## The Typical Homeschool Day and the Planes of Development

A typical day for a homeschooled child depends on where the child is on the planes of development and the knowledge the parent has in understanding those planes and making the most of the learning that is planned for the day, plus taking advantage of the learning that happens spontaneously. The parent becomes the architect and the engineer guiding the child into an environment where learning is beautiful and efficient. The parent then becomes the scientist by observing and recording the child's interests and progress. The parent has always been the teacher or guide as they teach children from birth how to crawl, walk, talk, feed themselves, take care of their body, and interact. This just needs to continue on to the next stages of development that the child experiences. This does not change. The same care and attention needs to be given to children to help them succeed in those later stages so they grow up into the adults they want to be.

## The Infancy Stage

**A child in the first plane of development**—also referred to as the infancy stage (birth to age six)—will be introduced to, get a chance to practice, and then want to completely attain physical and biological independence. They will naturally be curious about the world around them. A typical day for this child would be waking up on his own when well rested and, with the help of the parent, would get ready to start the day. For a child, getting himself ready (washing face, brushing teeth, getting dressed, brushing hair) is among the first skills to be acquired for everyday life. The same goes for meals, nap time, bath time, potty training, and bedtime. Children's curiosity and natural desire to want to see and touch everything are natural progressions, so providing an environment with accessible learning materials like wooden blocks, sorting activities, and puzzles will satisfy that developmental need and allow them to acquire mastery.

Art and music have a natural appeal to children as they affect the senses, so implementing these are very useful. Hands-on concrete materials like the Montessori materials are excellent for providing small lessons for acquiring fine motor skills, gross motor skills, practical life skills, sensorial skills for learning spatial recognition and vocabulary, basic math concepts, basic geography concepts, basic science concepts, reading, and writing. The practice of using these materials independently, which looks like playing, is how learning happens. Following observation, the parent takes note of the child's progress and will know when the child is ready for the next-level lesson. Time spent inside consists of accessing the concrete materials, learning life skills, and expressing love, care, and attention. Time is also spent outside, whether it's in the backyard or going to the grocery store, the bank, or the park, which can all be considered field trips that provide ample opportunities to learn and discover many different things. Playing outside in nature allows children opportunities to learn about botany, zoology, and astronomy. The children can collect specimens and, on the next trip to the library, check out books that connect the knowledge to their specimens. Socialization (more on this in Chapter 9) is learned via the parents' regular interactions with society, and it is the template that children copy, so demonstrating polite manners, explaining behavior, and showing conflict resolution are important for children to learn the correct social interactions. Emotional stability is learned by copying the parents, so being patient, understanding, caring, loving, and empathetic is key in helping children attain it successfully.

Again, technology is and should be used very minimally, even up to no amount at all. In addition to the negative impacts it has on child development, it affects attention span and makes it very difficult for books or other learning materials to compete. As engineers, we can marvel at and value technology, but we understand that a developing mind is not ready yet to handle the overstimulation and the responsibility skills that come with it. It's almost like handing over advanced technology to a more primitive human race that ends up disrupting their peace, which results in destroying them altogether; hence, they fail to make progress and advance, which would have been their natural evolution given the time and patience.

Instead of using technology—e.g., screens—instill the love of books by reading to children every day, especially at nighttime before bed; it becomes an enjoyable and valuable pastime. This creates a more positive impact on children as it can entertain or relax them and helps in forming a closer bond with you, which is necessary for them to want to continue to learn from you. The only structure for this age group is one that follows a schedule that aligns with the family's everyday living, where the times to wake up, eat meals, use the bathroom, and go to bed are consistent and in line with healthy development and, hence, healthy growth. Also, interestingly enough, at this development stage, playtime is learning, and learning is playtime.

## The Childhood Stage

**A child in the second plane of development**—also referred to as the childhood stage (ages six to twelve)—will be introduced to, get to practice, and want to completely attain mental independence. They will naturally want to acquire knowledge. They want to know almost everything about everything—appropriate to their maturity level, of course. A typical day for this child is similar to one of a child on the previous plane, but with the already-acquired physical and biological independence, they are anxious and ready to acquire mental independence. They want to know how the world works. This is the best stage to introduce the basic concepts of readiness for higher learning, to be presented later on in the next plane of development. The experiences in the first half (ages six to nine) lay the foundation for the second half (ages nine to twelve). How strong the foundation is and how well the concepts are learned in the first half will dictate how smoothly the next, more advanced concepts will be grasped in the second half.

This is a huge transition when you think about mathematics, for example. In the beginning, children learn mathematical operations with single-digit numbers, and by the end, they are solving simple algebraic equations. That is why it is so important to use concrete materials and allow children to master concepts concretely. Their minds are ready to learn advanced concepts presented in a simpler concrete way, but abstract information is too vague and has no meaning to them—not yet.

Anywhere around ages nine through twelve, children are ready for the transition to abstraction, when they can connect their mastery of concepts in the concrete form with their abstract form. If a child, for example, is able to explain how the equation for solving the area of a two-dimensional figure was derived, how it came to be in our history, and why it is useful for us to know today, then you have a child who has mastered this mathematical concept concretely and abstractly but, more importantly, knows it by heart and is able to teach it to another person. Compare that to a child who was only able to memorize the mathematical formula and complete the exercises but has no idea where it came from and what the point of learning it is.

Again, the time inside the home is spent using concrete materials that are tied to academic knowledge. The child will use the resources available, like books and documentaries, to learn the many interesting things they want to learn about. Continuing to introduce learning concepts in a fun and engaging way is key to keeping a child interested and wanting to learn more on their own. Music and art are pursued more passionately. Reading and writing become more advanced with practice and even more so when it is done with pure enjoyment.

We remember introducing poetry to our daughter. She was very interested but thought the Shakespearean sonnet was a bit too advanced until we learned the haiku. She soon learned how easy and fun it was to write haikus. She wrote them frequently—so frequently that she taught herself to contemplate and write down acquired wisdom at that age. She mastered the concept of poetry and especially the haiku. These experiences led to other learning breakthroughs. Our daughter has since studied philosophy and Japanese culture and language. This proves that children are capable of pursuing their interests that circle back to the importance of learning academics. They need to discover the importance of academics on their own while pursuing what they want to learn about at that particular moment in time. As parents, it is our job to facilitate that natural learning process to happen.

Technology is seldom introduced as a tool for learning and not for entertainment. Learning to write reports and presentations on the computer is time well spent and valuable for the future. An older child will understand the significance of technology and will have developed the responsibility for it. Time spent outside is still considered field trips, and the child is learning even more advanced skills. Their socialization skills and emotional stability are still being learned from copying the parent, so it is useful to be aware of the good and bad within ourselves as children become our mirror. Some children, toward the end of this plane, will start to slow down in their acquisition of knowledge when they feel satisfied as they are beginning to transition to the next plane of development. The only structure that exists consists of the family's everyday schedule and any extracurricular activities the child may have, such as music lessons, art lessons, or being part of a sports team.

## The Adolescence Stage

**A child in the third plane of development**—also referred to as the adolescence stage (ages twelve to eighteen)—will be introduced to, get to practice, and want to completely attain social independence. They will naturally want to do their own thing in their own way. Parents sometimes confuse this with the children being rebellious, but it's more that they have acquired even more independence and are now trying to figure out this socially constructed world they find themselves in. The children in this plane have already gained physical, biological, and mental independence. They could literally plug themselves into society and pick up what adults do, master even more skills, and acquire even more knowledge independently. They're still inexperienced, but they are not babies anymore, and they can stand on their own two feet. They will naturally want to know how society works, and sometimes that means challenging it, even in the home, to understand the boundaries. They will learn to judge people as they will see their flaws. They will see virtues in people and the lack thereof. They will see consistencies and inconsistencies. They will test how far the rules can be bent in order to get ahead and will also learn the consequences of certain decisions.

A typical day for this adolescent child can be very different from the earlier planes. In their biology, they will be experiencing hormonal imbalance as part of puberty, something that cannot be prevented. Their bodies being drained of energy as part of their metamorphosis will sometimes make it difficult for them to adjust to the normal family routine. Sometimes, more sleep and rest are required, and they will need to wake up later in the day. Having succeeded in the previous two planes of development, the child will now want to venture outside the home, make some connections with others, and gain even more experiences and independence. Even when not sure in the beginning, they will figure out eventually where they want to go in life. They will start to think about whether they want to continue with academic studies in order to attend college, apply for an apprenticeship in a specific skill, attend a trade school, own their own business and become an entrepreneur, or even just get a job and start earning a living. This child will have many thoughts and, through many discussions with the parents along with their support and guidance, will arrive at the decision of what path they want to be on to have the future they desire. The time spent inside and outside the home revolves around the path they chose, and the child will acquire the knowledge and hone the skills necessary on their own terms. Still abiding by the structure of the family schedule so as not to miss out on family time, the child will learn the balance between socializing, family, and responsibility. They will begin to acquire the time management skills to be successful and have a happy life.

Having a strong parent-child bond originating from the previous planes of development is what lays the foundation for understanding at this plane the difference between loving and non-loving relationships. Through these experiences of being in a loving home with loving parents and the trust that is built, they will have learned what to look for in others when they want to start their own loving families.

## The Maturity Stage

**Lastly, a child in the fourth plane of development**—also referred to as the maturity stage (ages eighteen to twenty-four)—will be introduced to, get to practice, and want to completely attain spiritual and moral independence. They will naturally want to know about spirituality and morality to understand themselves for the purpose of gaining self-awareness. They want to remain true to themselves and to their purpose in society. They will work on answering their own question on whether they've done everything within their power to attain a sense of total fulfillment. The quality of the parent-child bond developed in the previous planes of development will be revealed at this time by whether the children know they can still count on their parents for support in any way, they have no problem asking for help from their parents, and are comfortable having any type of conversations or discussions with their parents.

A typical day for this young adult is just like that of any other adult, whether still living at home or living on their own. The structure is built around the normal schedule of a healthy adult with good habits. After attaining so much independence, they want to challenge themselves with their own beliefs and morals. They will assess themselves and determine whether they are content with the state of things in their life. They will judge themselves and decide whether they are where they want to be physically, mentally, socially, and emotionally. They will even assess their relationship with their parents. That's the level of self-awareness that determines when a child has finally achieved maturity. They will complete the final plane by reaching full adulthood and will then have all the tools necessary for a successful, healthy, and happy life.

• • • •

For homeschooled children, the world is their oyster. There are unlimited resources for learning and free access to the outside world and society. Every trip outside the home is a field trip. Also, there is an unlimited amount of time to learn and the freedom to plan and execute the future they truly want. Nothing else exists that could provide this abundance of opportunities to ensure a successful future.

# CHAPTER 9

# What about Socialization?

"**B**ut what about socialization?" Every homeschool parent has received this insult disguised as a simple question from non-homeschooling parents and teachers before and often. In this chapter, you will learn how to respond to the question and demolish the false assumptions behind it. Because, regardless of the hype and fear we hear about homeschoolers and their need for socialization, most detractors have no idea what socialization is. That's why we always reply, "What do you mean by socialization?" to the question. We then hear the following answer with astonishing regularity: "You know, like . . . being around friends, playing football, and going to the prom."

It's obvious—they're confusing the psychological and developmental term *socialization* with an act of *socializing*. These two are distinct but often confused. A person's ability to socialize (interact with others) is a result of their developed socialization skills (ability to regulate and manage emotions and analyze behavior in the context of a society's functional norms). The American Psychological Association (APA) defines *socialization* as "the process by which individuals acquire social skills, beliefs, values, and behaviors necessary to function effectively in society or in a particular group."[47] Socializing is not that. So let's discern what socialization actually is in the real world—and the insidious propaganda elevating socialization as an essential goal for children in the minds of misguided parents.

# The Two Types of Socialization and the Usurpation of Parenting

In education, as in most specialized industries, the term *socialization* has a more nuanced definition and criteria than the one we use every day—and even more specific than the general psychological definition. In the education field, socialization is divided into two types: primary socialization and secondary socialization. The family environment, parenting, sibling and parent relationships are considered primary socialization. This includes the moral, cultural, and ethnic values that a parent wants to pass on. When people claim to show concern for socialization, they act as if primary socialization doesn't exist while homeschooling parents look at them with confusion—as if to say, "What am I, chopped liver?"

We homeschoolers recoil because this primary socialization has been the foundation of human civilization for all recorded history. The laws, rules, and moral codes of societies and cultures were derived from the institution of the family. It wasn't until the twentieth century that sociologist George Mead and his theory of social behaviorism claimed that the sense of self (self-image, self-awareness) is merely a product of a person's social experience. In addition, Urie Bronfenbrenner's ecological systems theory from 1964, which may rightly outline and categorize environmental pressures and inputs, failed by assuming a socialist, political "solution." The result of his appeal before Congress made parents subservient to a state education "environment," based on his premise that children fail in part because of deficiencies in their support system. Bronfenbrenner's half-truthful, half-baked theory was the catalyst for the 1965 Head Start program. The intent was to help break

---

47 "Socialization," APA Dictionary of Psychology, American Psychological Association, n.d., https://dictionary.apa.org/socialization.

the cycle of poverty by providing numerous childcare, preschool, social care, health-care, and other services. Yet there is scant evidence that the billions of dollars and millions of man-years over the last fifty-five-plus years have even put a dent in poverty improved quality of life, or overall academic success. [48,49,50]

However, both Bronfenbrenner's and Mead's contributions shed light on the secondary socialization type: i.e., social learning. This type of socialization is better defined as social *conditioning* or the process of training individuals to respond in a manner approved by their peer groups and society in general. Instead of parents and siblings, a child gets teachers and peers. A new set of artificial system rules is created—obey authority, accept arbitrary controls—and they are forced to associate with peers. Social context for navigating the system is like trying to explain bicycles to fish—except the system is unforgiving, brutal, and a breeding ground for bullies—both peers and teachers. Secondary socialization is precisely what they mean when they claim that homeschoolers are not socialized. They claim that their main objective is to make children socially competent and that children must develop these prescribed skills so they can function within the school setting, achieving their socially sanctioned goals. To me, it sounds like they want to tame children, rather than socialize them. [51]

We live in diverse societies—even *within* this country. This wasn't always the case—most of human history was made up of separate enclaves of cultures defined by borders or other geographical constraints. Within them, there existed sets of rules, laws, morals, customs, and courtesies that each culture defined for familiarity, communication, understanding, and harmony. For them, culture defined the society, and the root of that culture was the family. It was the family that played the primary role in creating the codes of conduct. Children were instructed by their families on conduct and behavior—but it was more than that. The conduct pointed to higher spiritual truths, whether of sky or animal spirits, great spiritual teachers, sun and moon gods, or organized religions. The priestly class of the last

---

48  Karen L. Robson, Sociology of Education in Canada (North York, Ont.: Pearson Education Canada, 2012), https://ecampu-sontario.pressbooks.pub/robsonsoced/chapter/__unknown__-6/#:~:text=A%20major%20objective%20of%20socialization,in-tellectually%20within%20the%20school%20environment.
49  Lillian Mongeau, "Is Head Start a Failure?" The Hechinger Report, August 9, 2016, https://hechingerreport.org/is-head-start-a-failure/.
50  "Primary Socialization," SparkNotes, n.d., https://www.sparknotes.com/sociology/socialization/.
51  Robson, Sociology of Education in Canada.

ten thousand years also helped mold societies' various codes. From the beginnings of human civilization, the family, the clan (extended family), and the church were the sole creators of culture and society. However, along came a new "priestly class" called *teachers*, and with the help of modern psychology and leftist sociology, they were ready to wrestle the traditional role of socialization (which is under the realm of parenting) from the family to a state institution called education.

Instead of dividing socialization into primary and secondary, let's simplify these terms:

> **Primary socialization** (a.k.a. parenting): The impartation of moral and ethical codes of values and principles that believes that the family is the functionality and arbiter of virtues. And those virtues are based on universal and transcendent principles.

> **Secondary socialization:** Social engineering and conditioning by those whose agenda it is to usurp and supplant the family and establish and perpetuate a system of power over parents and control of their children.

So there is parenting, and then there are social predators. This was true even under the Prussian model at its inception. They wanted to create a compliant population that would take orders from the state and not disobey when generals ordered them to face off with Napoleon's cannons specifically. There are now few cannons of the black powder and iron kind, but that doesn't mean there are no longer imminent threats to your children's future and your legacy. You can make your children immune to social conditioning and enable them to stand up to the social engineers, but it might take some hard work from you in examining your own foundation of socialization and in developing your parenting philosophy.

## "Am I Socialized?"

First of all, are *you* socialized? Socialized to what? Are we socialized (or conditioned) to function in a dysfunctional world? Does your mental health provide a healthy environment for your child's mind to develop? What was your childhood like? Was it full of stress and conflict? Did your parents fight and yell? How about their ability to control their emotions? What is your adverse childhood experience (ACE) score? Have you taken the Big Five personality traits test? Can you articulate your moral philosophy, and is it consistent with the rest of your values and goals? Are your personality and traits toxic to your children's mental and emotional development?

We have already shown that socialization and your family's values go hand in hand—they are not separate because socialization is parenting. Your job as a parent includes mastery of your stability, mind, and emotions *and* the ability to interact with others in a way that demonstrates that grace and resolve. It is only then that you can say you have reached and mastered your own socialization and are ready to guide your children properly. Whereas it can be a work in progress, you must embrace self-knowledge and the ability to navigate personal conflicts to de-escalation and resolution. If you cannot resolve disputes, you will create them.

Note that agreeableness is not socialization. To merely acquiesce to authority in order to "be nice" or resolve an issue is not teaching morals, values, and virtues. Avoidance of conflict can be just as psychologically painful as the conflict itself. Avoidance breeds resentment, and resentment can grow into hatred. Your ability to resolve conflict calmly and reasonably by considerate listening must be mastered and encouraged. The key to this mastery is (wait for it) the values, virtues, morals, and ethics you adhere to and have adopted as the basis for your family's socialization. Without a universal and transcendent set of principles/morals at the highest level, your philosophical center of how to navigate social situations, make judgments, and evaluate personal conflicts becomes haphazard. When we master ourselves, we master our social interactions—not as a manipulator, but as a *socialized* member of society.

## Beyond Socialization

We have explained that secondary socialization was an invention of institutional compliance training—a design feature of the Prussian model—and then justified by academics like George Herbert Mead and Urie Bronfenbrenner. We know that the social engineering and social conditioning of today (secondary) is not the natural, family-based socialization (primary/parenting) of most of human history. We can say with confidence then that:

- The idea that a child can be socialized in a system of compliance training is absurd.
- The homeschooling socialization argument is an attempt to condition people to accept the state and not the family as the cornerstone of society.
- Public schools do not offer any training in socialization—they only offer conditioning to accept dehumanization through stress compliance.
- It is ridiculous to think that cramming age-matched kids together in a prison-like environment for eight-plus hours per day is socialization.
- Primary socialization is just parenting.
- Primary socialization has been the norm for human civilization.
- Parenting includes the imparting of moral codes, values, virtues, and good judgment derived from universal and transcendent principles.

What does all this look like practically? How, as a parent, are you going to impart virtue and good judgment as socialization?

First off, we are not advocates of helicopter parenting as that robs children of their agency. We want children to develop and practice agency at various levels and milestones toward their own mastery. But we have to give them the templates and observational tools for judging what is good and bad. We know that at some point in the child's moral development, the parent's claim of good and bad suffices; however, after that point, a parent's mere claim does not hold the same weight—the claim has to be *tested* by the children themselves.

Children at all stages of development require appropriate levels of parental protection of mind, body, emotions, and nutrition to facilitate best growth and health development. So what do we do about the *other* children? When your child meets another child in the park, what is your level of concern? Do you watch them a bit to make sure there is no bullying? Do you see or look for the other parents? Lots of normal questions and observations are happening all at once. What is this? This is formally called *vetting*, and it's a normal, necessary part of parenting *and* socialization. Vetting your children's playmates may include getting to know the parents and other influences, such as siblings and other friends. Over time, your child will catch on to how you are protecting them by your approval of some children over others. Unfortunately, some parents flippantly say at a peer conflict, "Oh, let them just work it out themselves." This is the worst advice as it sends the message to your child that their upsetting conflict is not worth your time, and you also lose a chance to impart wisdom on conflict resolution to your child.

Vetting is an active-to-passive process of imparting demonstrable wisdom; vetting is not demanding specific behavior and life choices. Vetting is a tool and a skill like any other tools and skills to be handed over when maturity is mastered.

Vetting even includes the external environments in which your family operates. We must know and vet the people, the places, the shows, and the internet exposure that affect the development of our children. We are the firewall of their mind, emotions, and soul. Is this not also part of socialization? Yes! We are the protectors of our families, and part of that responsibility is to have standards and judge people and things on their values—we would be derelict in our parental duties if we accepted everyone as an influence on the psyches of our children. Parents need to vet their children's friends, their friends' friends, their friends' parents, their dates, and even their future spouses.

One major milestone in parenting is preparing your children for matrimony through the vetting of suitors and potential brides. They need a voice of reason, logic, experience, and maturity—don't leave it up to chance and whim. This is not simply *telling* your kids who to be friends with or who to and who not to date/marry. It's knowing that your role as a parent is to provide counsel when your kids come to you with questions about potential friends and suitors. It is explaining the moral intent behind who to choose and not choose as friends.

Vetting is instructional in defining your social groups. The worst thing to say is, "Whatever you want, honey, as long as it makes you happy"—this is non-advice, passively coercive, and contentious. The other extreme is authoritarian parenting approaches, in which the parent tries to control the child. These are the fastest two ways to guarantee your child ends up with—and later divorces—the wrong person.

## "Wait, I Thought Socialization Was, Like, Doing Stuff"

Talk to any long-time homeschooler, and they will have a long list of social activities that are not related to your local school district. Many towns have vibrant homeschooling communities and networks with lots to do and see. Local municipalities also have numerous sports activities like softball, soccer, fencing, et cetera. There are also paid activities like martial arts, sewing, quilting, cooking, and welding. The local community colleges regularly have their lifetime learning classes in everything under the sun. It is not uncommon for parents to take these classes with their kids. This type of interaction is not socialization per se, but the *practice* of socialization. Children practice their interpersonal relationship skills with the benefit of having their parents with them and not being stuck in school and bullied by peers and even teachers and administrators—you know the ones.

The hurdle many face is that they have been conditioned to believe that children need all this structure and structured play. Or they believe that every activity must have some meaning. Why can't we just take a walk in the woods, and every stick is either a sword or a gun? Maybe a gathering of leaves is a fairy's notebook, and a collection of pinecones become hand grenades. At some point, we need time to contemplate clouds and autumn leaves and socialize with our inner selves. Many times, this self-contemplation happens naturally out of what we commonly call boredom. Contrary to common belief, we think that boredom can be the stage right before creativity. It is the time when a child's own agency creates the game.

Speaking of agency, what happens when a child's natural love for learning becomes their new normal? What do you do when they are educating themselves? Is homeschooling . . . over?

Apply the radical new approach of this book, and you'll be seriously considering questions like these with your children. Let's address them now.

# CHAPTER 10

# Agency: The Heart of Self Education

Are you starting to see the elements of this radical new approach yet? If not, you will after this chapter. In the planes of development—specifically, the beginning of the third plane (twelve to eighteen years)—children enter a new relational dynamic and interaction with their parents. They become more independent just entering puberty. Your relationship with them will change, and you know you can't treat them the same as you did when they were eight or nine—these thirteen and fourteen-year-olds want to do things *themselves*.

Here we will reintroduce you to the term *agency*. Many people feel like they have no control over their lives—they may be suffering from crushing stress because they feel trapped in a world they have no control over. But how did they get there? How do children grow up to be adults and not develop agency? Well-developed agency means that a person has control over their life and allows for that individual to be able to act on their best judgment. We have mentioned agency in previous chapters, but let's now define it again.

*Agency* (psychological definition): the degree to which an individual has the ability to make decisions about their life.

To have agency means to have control or the feeling of control over your life and the decisions you make. Basically, am I free to make rational plans and decisions for my life, and do I have the ability to control and direct the outcome of those decisions? Or, *Can I do it? Can I own it? Hence, I am responsible for it.*

Agency comprises two things:

- A sense of agency
- A sense of ownership

The concept of *high* agency implies an active organism: one who desires, makes plans, and carries out actions. *Low* agency is hallmarked by a dissociation or an ambiguity between ourselves and the things we do or have done. However, learning and developing agency should not be skills that only begin at thirteen or fourteen years old—setting the stage and learning the basics of agency can begin even at age two or three.

In child development, low agency is commonly associated with an abusive or domineering environment—the harsher or more authoritarian the environment, the lower the agency that is developed. However, low agency within an abusive or domineering household can be a survival mechanism. It makes no sense to constantly confront an authoritarian parent who dictates every aspect of a child's life. For some children, it's easier to just go along with their parents' demands and avoid conflicts, whereas for others, it is common to *always* be confronting their parents. However the dynamics may be, the result of this is that the child is conditioned to do as they are told and is stripped of an important stage of development when they are just starting to practice their agency.

Ironically, a child may then exhibit obedience and compliance, which some parents might interpret as being responsible, but when the child is unsupervised, their behavior is anything but responsible. Other children may be able to keep up appearances for a while if they are particularly high in agreeableness, but if the seeds of agency have not been sown throughout all the developmental planes, being able to exhibit high agency will be a foreign experience for them. Regardless of where your child is on the agency spectrum, they can develop and nurture their own agency, and the third plane of development is your opportunity as a parent to supercharge it.

Remember, the Prussian model of education is not in the business of developing agency, but it is in the business of creating a compliance-based system to control people and populations. However, when we raise children who can make their own decisions, set their own goals, and have the freedom to choose a path, those children do not have a problem paying attention—so we could surmise that high agency may be associated with longer attention spans. In *Education and Peace*, Maria Montessori writes:

> The child who has never learned to work by himself, to set goals for his own acts, or to be the master of his own force of will is recognizable in the adult who lets others guide his will and feels a constant need for approval of others.[52]

Seeking constant approval as an adult is a hallmark of arrested development from childhood—these were the children who were never given agency. It is like an office worker who never takes responsibility for their actions but always blames others—these people were given no agency. They were always told what to do, and therefore the responsibility naturally fell on the manager, the team leader, the situation, the schedule, or the parent. They never think they are wrong because they were never taught that they could direct their own life and never understood the responsibility that comes with *ownership* of their life. They, instead, were taught that "being good (moral) is doing what you are told," and this is the philosophy that creates people who will walk in front of Napoleon's cannons or claim that their act of atrocity is "just doing their job."

You don't want that for your children—you want your children to learn how to direct their lives and make choices based on the values and virtues you instilled and not because they were *told* to do so, but how these virtues were *demonstrated*. This is why your relationship with your child will begin to change when they are thirteen or fourteen years of age—the seeds of agency are just now sprouting, and your parenting style, your homeschooling role, and your relationship must make room for this burgeoning agency. It's a

---

52  Maria Montessori, Education and Peace (Wheaton, IL: Theosophical Publishing House, 1949).

beautiful thing—and it will naturally make you nervous. But, if you can manage it, your workload with homeschooling will get lighter as the child's agency kicks in, and they are doing math, science, history, languages, et cetera all on their own initiative. At this point, you don't need to teach every lesson but just set forth a general guide and a plan with milestones.

Remember that children tend to pursue an interest for its own sake because their parents either encouraged them to or *discouraged* them from it. Either it was a natural desire that was cultivated, or coercion and control motivated the child to "rebel" and try their hand anyway. Agency is the reason our daughter finished three years' worth of middle school in a matter of eight months and many years before her peers, for example. We encouraged her to do so, and we did not "make" her do it. Her pride in her achievement gave her more confidence to continue challenging herself.

When children discover something is within their control, they are able to exercise agency over it. Unfortunately, children in authoritarian environments have their agency seized or expunged at every turn during their upbringing, and so various disorders may develop. For example, children who eat too much (or too little) are often exercising agency over the one thing their parents allow them to control—food. And the parent can't or won't tell the child not to eat. It's destructive yet preventable.

The bottom line is that you cannot micromanage your children into self-motivation and personal responsibility. Micromanaging parents do not allow children to discover creative ways of doing things. They suppress creativity and make tasks dull and boring. They rob children of their agency to the point where the child is afraid to trust even themselves. Micromanaging is just another name for authoritarianism. It may bring obedience, but it kills agency as agency does not develop at another's instruction or dictation.

## But How Do I Make Sure They Make the Right Decisions?

Now, at this point, you might have some understandable concerns about your child's agency and the decisions they make. What if they choose the "wrong" path, for example? Or forsake their studies entirely? These fears are, in fact, a valuable signal—*it's time to back off.* When you begin feeling this way, it can be an indicator of you wanting to strip them of the chance to practice their agency and start dictating their path.

Back in the 1990s, I (Jonathan) used to train German shepherds in Schutzhund part time—a hobby I truly enjoyed. One of the greatest feelings I got was when the dogs began to want to do things like tracking and obstacles—they were excited and anticipated their own favorite modules. Another older club member who had a permanent obstacle course at his large country place told me about one of his dogs. He would see this dog running on the course alone at first, then his other shepherds would join in. The more the man watched, the more he noticed that the one dog was *training* the other dogs—not as training, but as play. Just like that, you must break your preconceived idea that education is boring—that's your own mental malware. Instead, allow your children to discover the fun of different obstacles and stop tainting their first experiences of what difficulty is.

A common conflict that can occur between preteen or early teenage children and their parents is when the child is more interested in skills rather than in academics and they "have to" learn, according to their parents (or teachers). Don't sweat it—let them learn those skills because at the heart of all of those choices is an intact agency, but there is also another lesson that is being taught; you just have to have the patience to watch it be revealed. That lesson is time management. A lesson that says "You can't do it all today, so you need to plan out your days to maximize those skills." Ask yourself, "What does the child's planning lead to?" Do you see it yet? There doesn't need to be any conflict of wills here—just observation and guidance. In other words, don't sabotage their agency.

How do you know when the child is "there," at that friction point of a parent sabotaging their agency? It's when you get the eyeroll. And the all-to-common response, "I know, Mom." In the moments preceding that reaction, the parent has already stepped on the child's agency. You must realize that your relationship is changing and maturing. You cannot treat them the same way you did even just a couple of years ago. At thirteen or fourteen years old, children are well on their way to becoming independent young adults. That doesn't mean the child is a master of time management, but they don't want to be reminded of what they already know they need to do. Sometimes children adopt responsibility in a clumsy way, but adopt it nonetheless they must. Even a ten-year-old child should not have to be told to brush their teeth, for example. At some point, that handoff must occur. Just remember, being "responsible" for children is a subset and result of agency. It comes from being given the opportunity to practice their own independence without being micromanaged or coerced. Even a slave can be thought of as being "responsible" because they get all their work done, but that doesn't mean that they have agency because the slave has no control over his life.

# Now for the Hand-off: Conversations That Cultivate Agency

This third plane of development is your child's launch point to accelerate their learning faster than a parent or teacher can teach. When agency is involved, no obstacle is too large, no goal is too far off, and no dream is too big. When a child is doing what they choose to do, their development is unbounded, but how do parents get them to that point? What's a parent to do?

Around the age of ten through fourteen—most likely twelve or thirteen—specific parent-child conversations need to start occurring. What does the child, an independent learner in the making, wish to study? You can open the child's world up to the possibilities. Have those long and numerous chats about their future, about what they want to do in the world, what kind of person they want to marry, and how many children they want. Ask about their favorite car and what it will be like to drive it—and afford it. Ask about what type of man or woman they want to be and what type of parent and grandparent they would be. These are the conversations that will transform their simplistic, momentary views of the world into them *planning* their world. Simple prompts like this help the child consider what it will take to go from "kid living at home" to "successful adult with means."

These conversations will lead to other conversations on planning. For example, your child wants to learn the guitar. After all the fun conversations on how cool it would be to know how to play, all the different styles, the different string instruments, wait a few days. Then gather data on guitar lessons in your area and say, "Were you still interested in learning to play? I found some lessons in our area." But a word of caution—if they want to quit, find out why. Don't just blindly make them stick it out—that also strips them of their agency. Assess the situation and mentor them.

Maybe it's not playing the guitar; maybe your child wants to practice a certain profession. It's the same method as the guitar: you introduce the path of skills, lessons, and subjects they need and then have conversations. If failures happen, have conversations to assess the pitfalls and how to avoid them. If an area needs more attention, then yes . . . have more conversations. Remember, you are not *telling* the child what to do; you are a guide, a mentor, a person with life experience.

Unfortunately, even when parents understand the importance of a child's agency, they may still be stricken with panic because of the old mentality— that the successful path to college (or some other engrained paradigm) *must* be followed. To these parents, allowing children full freedom to be independent learners—meaning no grading, no testing, no lesson planning without the children's input or prompting—feels risky. But that is the heart of agency. Agency means you can trust the child to do what they are ready for when they are ready. They can accomplish what they want, if they want it enough. No force or coercion is needed from the parents. All you can do is support. Yes, you can influence and help assess risks. If parents still feel like they need to control the child's outcomes, then there is some self-reflection on the parent's part that needs to happen. We all hope that our children make the right decisions as they embark on their own journey, but if a parent is scrambling at the point of departure, it just means that the parent failed to prepare when they had the time. So maybe, just maybe, have lots of conversations about a future full of possibilities and hope.

Giving kids the big picture makes a lot of difference—this way, they can begin to make educated decisions for themselves. "Good general knowledge every citizen should know" is how you can frame what the state board of education requires your children to learn. Those conversations are not difficult once you, the parent, are having them.

What's difficult is being willing to have them. Give your child the knowledge to make choices and let their agency direct them.

In many ways, this radical new approach is made up of elements from not only the pre-Prussian ways but also from other family-based ways of teaching—e.g., the Montessori method, a bit of unschooling, a dip into psychology, a foundation of peaceful parenting, and agency building.

Let's recap the basic elements of our radical new approach to homeschooling:

- Homeschooling *is* parenting.
- A good parent-child relationship is paramount.
- Peaceful parenting—stop relying on aggression, coercion, and manipulation.
- Parents are the template—model the virtues you want to pass down.
- Discipline is regular practice toward mastery, not punishment.
- Teach to mastery, not to a grade.
- Prepare the environment for optimal learning and excitement.
- Learn to answer the "What's in it for me?" question.
- Understand the three pillars of pedagogy: philosophy, methodology, and observation.
- Gain proficiency in Montessori's four planes of development.
- Curriculum is just information—the information you tailor to your children.
- Read early; read often. Family reads together.
- External motivation is merely coercion and manipulation—that's why it doesn't work.
- Internal motivation is just motivation, and it's a product of having agency.
- A child who develops their own agency will be prepared for the future.
- Cultivate agency—not just for your children, but for yourself.

- Lay out a clear and understandable path from home education to life preparation.
- Primary socialization (parenting) is what matters most.
- Tailor the education by considering the learning styles of your children, the levels of mastery they want to acquire, and the homeschool style that appeals to them.
- Homeschooling can be affordable and flexible.
- Learning happens all the time.
- Mistakes are part of the learning process.
- Foster experimentation and discovery.
- Facilitate the mastery of concepts via concrete materials, then apply the passage to abstraction.
- A peaceful, happy, and stress-free home is conducive to learning.
- Have many meaningful conversations with your children to get to know them and to mentor them.

This radical new approach to homeschooling gets your children ten years ahead of their peers—these are the peers who are exiting college and still trying to figure out what they want to specialize in. Children who have been told what to do their entire lives will not know yet what they want to study. But with agency, children will want to be able to command themselves and guide their own future.

When a child reaches the age of competence and no longer needs others to teach them, they then need those people to act as guides and mentors. Mastery, at that stage, is just a bit further ahead, and they don't need a teacher for that. They just need practical application in the real world for feedback and adjustment. Don't worry too much if they enter the third plane of development a little late. Just adjust accordingly—delays don't matter. Only gaining competency in the end matters.

# CHAPTER 11

# What Does Your Child's Future Hold?

We've established that homeschooling transitions from home education to life preparation. This means less directed study and more self-exploration. With each passing year, children gain more and more autonomy to "do their own thing." Some teenage children may even be ready for their first job, micro-entrepreneurship, or college-level classes (if they have interest in or have motivation for academic study). We do not adhere to the disingenuous "college is for all!" hoopla as it is a fact that some occupations still require a college degree or advanced degrees. Think engineering, medicine, law, and other similar occupations. Your homeschooled child, having developed agency, will know this and will be ready for that challenge. Out of their own volition, they will seek out the right path and advice to achieve their higher-learning goals. They will not just go to college and waste four-plus years floating around prerequisite classes, getting Cs, and having an undeclared major.

That being said, we're not implying your child *should* take college classes at a local school, transfer to a four-year college when they're eighteen or nineteen in order to get a bachelor's degree, and eventually get a "real" job where they work for forty years. College is an option; it's not the *way* anymore. We no longer live in that world. In fact, the overwhelming majority of humanity throughout history didn't live in that world. The college-to-career pipeline is a recent invention, and it's already obsolete as a prerequisite for most people who want to have a successful career or want to start their own business. The internet and new technology have brought opportunities to anyone with a work ethic. Academic institutions, from your local public school to the Ivy League, haven't come to grips with this new reality yet. Elementary schools and universities alike are unable to guarantee success in life and work, much less give children anything close to a "good" education. The US school system is still struggling to maintain even the most basic literacy and mathematics benchmarks relative to the rest of the industrialized world.

A degree doesn't necessarily lead to a successful and fulfilling job anymore. However, anyone with a little motivation and a reliable internet connection can create their own job, grow a business, and then hire college-educated professionals to scale the company and create incredible profit for its owner—your child. Also, the future is owned and led by freethinkers and risk-takers—not salarymen and cubicle occupying citizens. We can even foresee a time when a college degree is a disqualifying factor for the very best job opportunities at the most cutting-edge companies in favor of applicants who have run several of their own companies, albeit on a smaller scale.

Let's return from the future to your child now, in the present day, and their education. Let's address what you can expect from your child as they begin exercising personal agency. What does future building look like for him? What do the next few years leading up to ages eighteen to twenty look like when agency is their superpower?

# Getting Ten Years Ahead of Their Peers (No Tiger Moms Required)

As we have said, our radical new approach to homeschool education gets your children ten years ahead of their peers. Those peers will be exiting college without direction, still trying to figure out what they want to specialize in. Many will be deep in debt, with no prospects for employment. Many will fail to launch, returning to (or never leaving) home, where they remain until Mom and Dad have enough and kick them out somewhere around ages twenty-eight to thirty-two. We can moralize all we want about what these young adults should have done, but when have you heard someone discussing the role of parents in their kids' future?

We can't really lay *all* the blame on these directionless young people, however. Consider how pathetic career guidance is at the high schools and colleges. Guidance counselors' anemic advice is legendary and comical to the point that it gets lampooned in pop culture. Mr. Mackey from *South Park* is the best known. His character is funny and relatable because Mr. Mackey is the embodiment of the guidance counselor stereotype.

Grades and extracurriculars give little to no opportunity for the child to discover what they love to do or what they're naturally good at, much less explore it to a meaningful depth. Not only that, but the child only gets to meet with the counselor a few times such as when they are close to graduation. This is usually when it's not enough or far too late to set a course. These students should have had those conversations at the earlier ages, practicing the development of life-goal pursuit and achievement throughout the different planes of development.

Now contrast the sorry state of modern career guidance with the past. What were children planning to do with their lives pre–Industrial Revolution? What about the post–Industrial Revolution? What skills did they have? What apprenticeships were available? I'm not saying we should all give up modern conveniences and become manual laborers. Simply consider that today's schools do not prepare children to *function* in this world, much less thrive as well as home-taught, self-taught, pre-internet societies did. How can we recapture that spirit? In the information age, the age of learning on the go, when skill mastery via YouTube alone is possible, we are realizing that we're no longer hindered by ivory-tower academia. Our new and manufactured reality is where newspapers print fake news; schools provide fake education; the media feeds us fake entertainment and sells us fake outrage. Reject their manipulation and break away from their mental malware—this is the mindset of those who succeed.

Speaking of manipulation, there is a breed of parents that push their children to get ahead through force, intimidation, shaming, coercion, and all manner of methods for their children to achieve. These are the Tiger moms and Tiger dads who have their own brand of robbing their children of agency. While we hear about some children who endure this type of abuse and self-erasure, we rarely hear about the failures and burnouts that are far more common. It's natural for parents to want their children to have a better life, but it is an entirely different dynamic to manufacture an abusive environment to achieve it. This is why promoting your child's agency and independence is far more effective. Besides, it is far more likely that the skill sets your child needs are not the ones from your own generation.

## Future Opportunities That Are Yet to Be

Your child's future occupation doesn't exist yet, and when it does, it will be so flexible that it will span multiple industries. Your child will be able to master multiple things—each of which you think they could make a living with, but your kid will just say, "Meh, I can always do that if I get bored." It's also possible that your child's agency-fueled motivation to innovate will create a new six- to seven-figure occupation. Don't quash agency—it's a superpower!

In keeping with the theme of the last chapter, we continue our discussion of agency as it is the heart of this radical new homeschooling plan, after all. It *must* include this magic called *agency*. That's why parents must stop the traps and snares they themselves place in front of their children, especially as they age into the independent-learning years. These traps are the old ways of doing and thinking. We'll share a quick example from Jonathan's life.

Early in my engineering career, I did a lot of contract-based jobs. I'd work on a project for six or twelve months, then move on to the next contract.

An old tool-and-die maker I was chatting with one day who had worked at the same shop for forty-two years asked me, "Can't you hold down a job?" The old guy just didn't get it. That baby-boomer mentality—get a degree, comb your hair, offer a firm handshake, and you'll get a good job—just didn't comprehend the fast-paced nature of engineering design work.

Now consider this new era—why a common career that young adults want now is "social media influencer." They recognize the opportunity the internet brings them to show off their skills, they get paid for them, and there's not a one-size-fits-all model. Honestly, I have trouble wrapping my head around how social influencers make a living. However, I have to think about a new, faster-paced world—an internet age in which learning on the go with available resources happens in weeks, days, even hours—not years. It's truly a world without grades, only mastery. A child may even be able to get paid for mastery before they turn ten years old. Because we live in a fast-paced, changing world where busy people don't have time to take classes, they call on masters of their domain to help them or just hire people to do things for them. This is not like any career path taught by our clunky, industrial-age school system.

## Laying the Path of Success

Consider again that "influencer" career. A person can be and do anything! They can monetize just about any hobby or passion—something impossible just a few years ago. As exciting as the possibilities are for having that live-streaming Minecraft channel, parents can get excited prematurely, and that can be a turnoff. We sometimes find ourselves automatically thinking about monetizing their burgeoning skills. They may not be there yet. Some children may not even want to monetize their skills right away and instead get a traditional job, like working at the local bookstore or coffee shop. That may or may not last very long. That's part of the learning process. Other children may have a different, non-internet skill set like an interest in cooking or baking. Parents can help these skills flourish by getting to know some local bakers and asking if they'd be interested in taking on an "apprentice" for a few days for some hands-on learning—just remember to follow the interests of the child. Maybe start a cottage business in which you can sell your product at a local farmers' market. For example, our daughter is the brand representative for our family business at the farmers' market. She wears the same outfit as she appears in on the product label. We don't force her to do anything; she does the work in the company that she finds fun, like promoting the product, meeting new people, befriending them, et cetera. She even used her connections to expand the business to include wholesale to other vendors—we now sell vanilla in bulk to another local food product manufacturer. It's old-school entrepreneurship, and it works. She doesn't talk about getting a job; she talks about hiring people! She thinks now in terms of capital and labor and has even had to negotiate to pay her mom to clean her room for her as a serious offer. Talk about a paradigm shift!

The great irony is that the internet has allowed us to recreate the business environment as it was for families and children a hundred years ago, a thousand years ago. But all you need is a website now; you don't need a storefront anymore. It's no longer the case that a child needs only one job, career, or business. It's having portfolio income and multiple sources of revenue to manage risk in their livelihood and in their future.

An important lesson to teach children (or allow them to learn on their own) during these apprenticeship years is to secure multiple eggs in multiple baskets (side hustles) that can flourish, particularly within the homeschooling community. That manages risk for each income stream and grants freedom to the family. A blind dedication to academics such as in traditional schools withholds all these opportunities from children. Imagine, however, your childhood and later formative years, switching from one income opportunity to another, seeing what works and what doesn't, and preparing for survival and success. Having that one stable job was OK at one point in history, but now, in the blink of an eye, everything can be taken away. Your employer, with the help of the government, owns you and your life and, as we have seen with the rollout of government mandates during the pandemic, will violate the law at your expense. We can even be subject to cancel culture—e.g., being fired for a garden-variety opinion shared on social media. That's no way to live.

Making money anywhere and in any way is the most important practical life preparation lesson children (and we) can learn and master. With an abundance mentality and a growth mindset, they will be able to see money and potential everywhere. They can have products or services to sell and then seize opportunities by saying, "Oh, I can do that. I can do more." There will come a point when they won't even need your encouragement; they will instead encourage *you* to do more.

However, the education system is six versions away from where we are. It's like using MS Word 97 rather than the most advanced word processing and AI content–generators available today. It's sad, really, that all modern education systems do, even through college level, is prepare people to become modern slaves unable to take care of themselves.

We and our children need to be able to survive in our education and careers by having the following skills. To become able to meet opportunities with preparedness—some call this luck, but this is the simple truth. Next, we need to become versatile, which is just having ability and willingness. Then we need to achieve the skill of reading with high comprehension and speed. After that, we need to achieve the ability to know where to find information. Next, we need to know how to network and partner with trusted and skilled people. Finally, we need to learn how to self-teach to full mastery.

With these few skills, your children can do anything in any industry from anywhere—the world is theirs, and the competition is almost nonexistent because they were homeschooled, peacefully parented, and given their agency. It's an amazing thing.

# CHAPTER 12

# Housekeeping, Bookkeeping, and Homeschool Laws

"But you're not qualified to teach" is a common accusation used against parents by public school teachers, educators, policy wonks, and ivory-tower academia. They say they are the experts, after all, and are far more knowledgeable about educating kids than parents. But there is a ruse in their highfalutin self-aggrandizement—one they don't think we'll catch.

Teachers are trained to teach large groups and to manage populations of kids, year in and year out. They're taught to handle interpersonal conflicts where they are required to manage multiple and varied demographics of children. That's not what homeschoolers do—we only have to understand our own children and impart the knowledge they need accordingly. Parents don't have to be experts in *all* children—just their own children. Parents also just so happen to be fully invested in their children's success. A schoolteacher can't devote that amount of time to just your kid; they're too busy. Because of that, professional teachers cannot be the experts—we, the parents, are the experts. Furthermore, teachers have no vested interest in our children, our families, or our values. There is not only no alignment; there is *mis*alignment.

Another truth about education professionals hidden in plain sight is that in most cases, we, the parents, have already completed their system. We went to school and graduated! Many parents have advanced degrees, professional training, and acquired life experiences. Some parents run businesses and have trained coworkers or employees. Remember, a teacher is primarily trained to teach large groups in specific, controlled environments. Homeschooling is a horse of a different color. We've been through their meat grinder and are privy to the same information our children will need to be introduced to.

A third gem of knowledge is that we parents did not need professional teachers to teach our children to crawl, walk, eat solid foods, dress themselves, brush their teeth, wash their bodies, use the potty, count, read their first words, know their shapes, and so many things necessary in early life. Why not continue this winning streak and continue teaching our children for the remaining years? Unfortunately, it has become all too common for parents to think that this responsibility should be outsourced to other people—hired hands, professionals, the so called "experts."

"But teaching a child how to walk is easy compared to subjects like history or algebra," you might say, but is it? Didn't you get a B in algebra, and you hated it? Didn't you even say, "How come Mr. Sandberg makes algebra soooo boring?" Weren't you also a student tutor for lower classmates in algebra? The fact is that parents who lack confidence will notoriously sell themselves short and believe this false narrative that since they believe that they can't teach their kids, you can't teach your kids. The reality is that you *can* teach and guide your child in *every* subject all the way up to graduation. There are, however, a couple of things you need to know on your homeschooling journey.

## Your Path to Being the "Expert"

### Step 1: Begin with State Laws

One thing we want to convey in this chapter is that you need to prepare yourself. Don't just wing it without knowing the basics of your state's laws on homeschooling. However, it's not that difficult to get started, and since the pandemic, it has become much easier to find the homeschooling information for your state. Each of the fifty US states has different requirements, and they all differ in the level of regulations. Some states have no or few regulations, and others have moderate to high regulations. Some states have education as part of their state constitutions while, in other states, the laws cover how much oversight and control they have over the education of children. Once you learn and understand how much oversight and control your state has, you will be able to provide what is needed and meet the requirements for you to homeschool your children in the state in which you reside.

For example, some states might just require a letter of intent to homeschool that a parent must send to their local school board, district, or superintendent. The parent may need to go through a qualification course if they don't have a college degree or enough college credits. Other states require certain records to be kept and annual assessment testing to occur. Still other states with higher regulations may even require the students to be assessed annually by a certified teacher. As you can see, the rules vary, so the sooner you find out what you need to do to legally homeschool your child, the sooner you will be on the right path. Don't worry if you need help; you can always find other homeschoolers and resources in your area that can guide you and provide you with much-needed assurance. Networking with other homeschoolers will become a very valuable resource.

## Step 2: Know What Records to Keep

Even though it may not be required in some states, we highly recommend doing some record keeping—at least to keep track of your child's progress and interests. It could be as simple as making entries in a planner or journal about what the child worked on with some assessment of mastery level. Your records are your records—you own them, and only you need to understand them. However, you may decide on a particular system as you get the hang of recording. If you are starting homeschooling when your children are very young, you will discover that records like transcripts are not as important. Some people may record when something is introduced, when something is still being worked on, and whether something has been mastered. This is common in Montessori, where records have the statuses of introduction, working and mastered on the different goals set for that child. This is appropriate for young children up to age twelve, and it lets you know when they are ready to be introduced to the next item in the sequential order.

The records provide parents with the sense that they are on top of things as they become experts in their child's learning experiences. Remember, record keeping is merely a tool, and it should be one that helps you with your homeschooling—tailor it to anything you need it to be. It can be a planner, a journal, or a more advanced form like an Excel spreadsheet or even an access database—it all depends on your comfort level. This will give you the practice and confidence needed for the later years in middle school and high school, when the record keeping will need to be more specific and official for those children interested in college admission.

When your child is about twelve years old beginning to enter into the third plane of development (ages twelve to eighteen) and they have been homeschooled all their life, you as the parent will be able to tell whether they are academically inclined or not. You will know whether they are capable of and still want to continue to learn the academic subjects to grasp the more advanced concepts or not. Record keeping for the child in the third plane of development depends on the path chosen for the future. For the parent who has a child who wants to attend college, the child's records will be similar to any high school or middle school student's—except you are the child's school, and you are putting together their transcript. We recommend learning about your local high school graduation requirements to help guide you in setting up the high school academic learning plan. Also, get in contact with the colleges of interest and find out what they require for admission—many are homeschooler friendly because they know that homeschoolers are typically high in self-reliance and possess high initiative. Some community colleges and universities offer high school diplomas and other opportunities to enter college early during the last two years of high school with some coordination with the public school system. There are still many options available at this stage. The record keeping for high school will generally include putting together the following things for your homeschool education:

- Transcript (The list of all the student's coursework taken and grades/levels achieved, and the studen'ts GPA)

- Syllabi (An outline of the objectives and subjects in a course of study)
- Course descriptions (A brief summary of a course, its rationale and key content)
- Homeschool Mission Statement (A document that describes your homeschool and its mission)
- Student Experience Letter (A letter written by the student that describes his homeschool experience)
- Test Records (SAT/ACT/PSAT scores, or any other assessment test records)

Checking with the college or university will help narrow down what is needed and what is not needed for admission. Again, network with other homeschoolers in your area, and they can provide much useful information as some of them may have already walked on the path you are now trying to get on. There's also a myriad of information online for homeschoolers with free examples and templates on how to put together any record-keeping documentation. The more resources you have at your disposal, the smoother the journey will be.

For the parent of a child who wants to walk a more independent path, the record keeping can continue the same way as the earlier years, but we highly recommend you adopt the official record-keeping format just in case your child decides to attend college later on. It is also a little-known secret that homeschoolers can issue their *own* homeschool diplomas. These homeschool diplomas are just as valid as the local high school diplomas as both are supported by transcripts, and proper transcripts accompanied by the other supporting documentation are a legitimate assessment of the work and study that was performed.

There are more opportunities available now than ever before. Children also have the option to attend trade school, start an apprenticeship program, learn entrepreneurship, or obtain employment. It will benefit families greatly if they realize that attending college is not the only choice available— that it is not for everyone and that it is no longer a guarantee of success. College has become a very expensive investment, sometimes without much of a return. Many young adults get discouraged, choose the wrong major, struggle financially with college debt, fail to graduate, or do not achieve the kind of success they anticipated. Entrepreneurship, on the other hand, has become more popular with the advances in technology, and there are many success stories of young entrepreneurs and their businesses. Children who gain independence early on and acquire high agency are capable of becoming successful in many nontraditional ways. They understand the difference between being employed by others and being self-employed.

A child who wants to attend a trade school can do so as early as high school, so getting in touch with the trade school of choice will help with fine-tuning the child's goals. Those who enter apprenticeship programs and/or want to be entrepreneurs will be directly learning those skills, and record keeping becomes keeping track of their accomplishments and/or certifications.

Are you seeing a pattern here? Your job as the homeschool parent also includes being the school counselor and career advisor. You are in charge of networking and advocating for your child's future. You will be calling and interacting with a lot of people, and some of them will be helpful while others will be rude and obnoxious.

But you shouldn't care—your sons and daughters would have become high-quality and highly skilled homeschooled champions, and on every call you make, the other people on the line will be hearing all about it.

# CHAPTER 13

# The Uncertain Future

Homeschooling doesn't just mean you teach your children at home for their sake. Homeschooling is a multigenerational and intergenerational activity. Our radical new approach results in homeschooled children desiring to homeschool their own children one day and continuing to do so for generations to come. That means you're passing down more than information. You're passing down your values and your family's own culture—your legacy. This matters because we're in a culture war. Education is the battlefront. In any conflict, the side that wants to win will beat the side that wants to be left alone. So homeschooling is more than teaching; it's an act of war against ideologies and the ideologues possessed by those who would, given the opportunity, target your children to steal, kill, and destroy them, spiritually, psychologically, or even physically. The tenets of the enemies of Western civilization claim they *must* destroy the family or, to use their terms, "dismantle" and "abolish." In the past, the easiest fight to win was to control where children learn, who teaches them, and what information they learn and that is what they have been doing. But, who are *they*?

There are a lot of folks that read the news about the "culture war" and they have no frame of reference as to what it's all about. Many react to some unbelievable headlines and think, "Why do they want to teach *that* in school?" The reasons, the Marxist say, for wanting to dismantle the family is that it remains the core attribute of western civilization against them. Marxism as an economic theory has been abandoned for a new cultural Marxism as of the 1950s till now. The Marxist realized that the proletariat was happy with Capitalism and could not be swayed to revolution, so they changed tactics towards social issues as a vehicle for revolution. The Frankfurt School acolyte, Herbert Marcuse (and others) called for new agents of revolution to be the legions of victim class peoples and/or political agendas/movements and the multitude of 1960s counterculture activists that target Western Civilization.[53] Regardless of the shift in tactics, Marxism has always been about the call for the abolition of the family as, according to them, perpetuates class inequality and the acceptance of hierarchy.

This culture war has targeted the institution of The Family for 150 years but has been going full steam since the 1960s. We have been under attack on many fronts, and it seems their forces have all but won. However, with one generation of homeschooling, families can turn the tide of the culture war and even win it for all that is good, true, and wholesome. To be able to recapture the institution of The Family through homeschooling is the loudest "bang for the buck" from a cultural, social, political, and economic perspective. And you don't have to spend 20 years fighting the school board or risking your kids in hopes they would "be a light in the darkness." Home education coupled with peaceful parenting is therefore the most significant civilization-wide activity any parent can do. Every family counts. After all, any issue needs only 3.5 percent participation to change everything; only 3.5 percent of parents who homeschool and peacefully parent can save Western civilization by creating a bulwark not of mere individuals but of connected

---

53  Marcuse, Herbert. The New Left and the 1960s: Collected Papers of Herbert Marcuse, Volume 3 (Herbert Marcuse: Collected Papers). New York, NY: Routledge, 2005.

and extended families whose ties are not easily broken.[54] Homeschooling's objectives reach far—they not only become the center of values and virtues in your own family, but they also establish communities of shared interest and reestablish strong local moral character.

Even so, the benefits of homeschooling are broader than the long-term protection of family values and defeat of poisonous ideologies of the many political movements and groups of what the marxists have absorbed. For most of civilization, the education of children has been the domain of parenting—the raising of children with virtues and values, and for them to learn skills or a trade. Government-sponsored education was the outsourcing of that responsibility. Homeschooling, then, is the recapturing of parenting. So for the last 150 years, the education of children has been ceded to the State till we can't even imagine how children learned math, reading, history, and science without the government placing a perpetual lien on people's homes called property taxes. Even though it is different from state to state, as a general rule, schools are funded almost exclusively by property taxes and almost all property taxes (percentage) go to schools—and the tax is levied regardless if you have paid off your home. In fact, the government can seize your home for not paying the property taxes. However, government schools justify their budgets by student headcount and municipalities in whole or in part, derive property tax levels on school budget demands. This means that mass homeschooling can provide the justification to end the perpetual property taxes for good and families will never again have to worry about property tax seizures—they will truly own their homes.

And what do all these taxes get us? We know how low the United States ranks in math/science/reading according to the OECD/PISA performance in comparison to other industrialized nations.[55] If it was only low PISA rankings, that might be one thing. Open indoctrination into Marxism (i.e., socialism), social emotional learning (SEL), comprehensive sexual education, critical theories (e.g., critical race theory), Common Core, gender theory, and numerous other mass social engineering initiatives have, over the last several generations, resulted in a programmed, divided, and dumbed-

---

54   David Robson, "The '3.5% Rule': How a Small Minority Can Change the World," BBC, May 13, 2019, https://www.bbc.com/future/article/20190513-it-only-takes-35-of-people-to-change-the-world.

55   Barshay, Jill. "What 2018 PISA International Rankings Tell Us about US Schools." https://hechingerreport.org, December 16, 2019. https://hechingerreport.org/what-2018-pisa-international-rankings-tell-us-about-u-s-schools/.

down society. Internet slang has a few descriptors for these individuals, who make up the vast majority of the general public, that include "normies" and "NPCs," referring to non-player video game characters who are unable to say or do anything beyond what the game's program has stipulated.

And if that's not bad enough, we're in a civilizational collapse. Many saw this coming prior to the last pandemic. It's probable that we will experience many instabilities into a bleak future for decades to come. We need to prepare ourselves and our children for it. Civilization itself is unstable and vulnerable right now, tipping ever further toward the brink of irreversible destruction. Here's what to expect:

- Economic downturns that don't self-correct
- The end of small- and medium-size farms as a result of worldwide climate initiatives
- More civil unrest and the continuation and escalation of global wars
- Supply chain issues with critical infrastructure products such as medications, computer chips, raw materials, and basic necessities that were outsourced to foreign countries like China and India decades ago
- Additional and irreversible inflation as governments borrow and print money
- Energy costs skyrocketing from scarcity (electricity, gasoline, diesel, natural gas)
- Food costs and food scarcity
- More lockdowns for pandemics and for climate agendas
- Travel restrictions for a Chinese Communist Party–style social credit system
- Transportation and shipping restrictions—regional, national and global logistics
- Unemployment and jobs market
- Collapsing banks and rising interest rates

However, homeschooled kids will be accustomed to rapid change, spontaneous and flexible schedules, problem-solving, and having agency-based initiative. They're able to survive and thrive under uncertainty and make decisions accordingly. Publicly schooled students are not used to disruption of their prescribed programming as they tend to wait for instructions—we see this even in adults with their own jobs. Does the average millennial or Gen Zer have basic skills like gardening, camping, carpentry, welding, child care, firearm skills, animal husbandry, basic first aid, or even cooking without a microwave? Now, I understand that each generation tends to complain about the next generation, but the reason you are reading this book is to equip your children for the uncertain future with the tools that homeschooling brings to bear in spades. We have shown you that homeschooling beats public education in academics, that it's cheaper, faster, and more efficient. This is so much so that the important life skills are not pushed out of the way by mounds of homework. Homeschooling internalizes problem-solving skills, which are increasingly essential in a rapidly changing uncertain world; this makes them strong in hard times, and hard times are coming.

The good news: you are not alone. More and more families will transition to homeschooling as they already have. As of 2022, there are 4.3 million homeschoolers in the United States, a major increase from the 1.9 million in 2019. Considering that public school enrollment in the same period went from 47.1 million to 40.2 million, homeschoolers are poised to become a tangible political force. That is good and bad. At a certain percentage of the whole, (statistically around 20 percent) the system, the status quo, will really fight back.

But before then, the positive influx of goods and services from the emerging homeschooling market will continue to fuel its own infrastructure. This means more resources for you. This will make your homeschooling experience better and easier. The more mainstream homeschooling becomes, the more favorable and accommodating the already homeschool-friendly colleges and universities will be. Politically, if we have 10 to 20 percent of the school-aged population at home, what can we demand on the issue of property taxes? It is not inconceivable that we will begin to hear about their abolishment. Does that sound too far fetched? Well, it's already happening.

In October 2022, Governor Greg Abbott of Texas said his goal was to eliminate school property taxes so that Texans can "genuinely own their own home without being taxed out of it."[56] Some may think this is just political hyperbole at this point, but it is being discussed and that is a good sign.

# The Empire Strikes Back

However, the detractors among our representatives and in global governance and academia are firmly entrenched—even in the United States Republican party, often viewed as the pro-family party. When we start from the premise of what freedom is—the clause in the Declaration of Independence that mentions "life, liberty, and the pursuit of happiness," it is clear that freedom is a life free from government involvement and harassment—that the government be merely a protector of our preexisting, intrinsic rights, not a life filled with permits, licensing, permission slips, authorization, regulations, compliance, and all other pseudonyms for government controls. Some may argue the need for various regulatory measures; the principle of freedom remains the same: you don't need the permission of others to live your life the way you want to live it. It is not my intention to lay out the entire picture of the opposition—that's for you to guard—but I will give you some of the players. Never assume these are isolated cases; these people operate in their multitude of organizations, think tanks, associations, and nongovernmental organizations (NGOs). Here are a few of the more well known who preach and strategize against the family, parental rights, and homeschooling:

- In 2013, MSNBC personality Melissa Harris-Perry did a Public Service Announcement stating that "We have to break free from the private idea that kids belong to the parents . . . but that kids belong to whole communities."[57]

---

56  Erin Anderson, "Texas Governor Commits to 'Eliminate School Property Taxes,'" Texas Scorecard, October 4, 2022, https://texasscorecard.com/decisiontexas/texas-governor-commits-to-eliminate-school-property-taxes/https://texasscorecard.com/decisiontexas/texas-governor-commits-to-eliminate-school-property-taxes/.
57  Ari Armstrong, "Melissa Harris-Perry Says Your Kids 'Belong to Whole Communities,'" The Objective Standard, April 8, 2013, https://theobjectivestandard.com/2013/04/melissa-harris-perry-says-your-kids-belong-to-whole-communities/.

- In 2019, renowned Harvard law professor Elizabeth Bartholet wrote a professional paper entitled "Homeschooling: Parent Rights Absolutism vs. Child Rights to Education & Protection," in which she frames homeschoolers, and specifically Christian families, as abusive, racist, misogynistic, radicalized, and indoctrinating their children—and that's just in the abstract.[58]

- In 2017, James Dwyer, law professor at the prestigious William and Mary College, stated that "The reason parent-child relationships exist is because the State confers legal parenthood," and "The State needs to be the ultimate guarantor of a child's well-being—there's just no alternative to that."[59]

- In 2015, Rob Reich, professor of political science and education at Stanford University, wrote concerning a federal tax credit for homeschoolers: "I see no problem with a federal tax credit. But a tax credit for homeschooling should not be offered without a requirement that homeschooled families accept some oversight."[60]

- In June 2020 and again in 2021, Harvard hosted summits on regulating homeschooling.[61] Of course, all three—Elizabeth Bartholet, James Dwyer, and Robert Reich—were in attendance, discussing concerns, reform proposals, regulatory oversight, political action, equity, social outcomes, and litigation strategies to oppose homeschooling and parental rights.[62]

---

58  Elizabeth Bartholet, "Homeschooling: Parent Rights Absolutism vs. Child Rights to Education & Protection" Arizona Law Review 62 no. 1 (2020), Harvard Public Law Working Paper No. 19-23, https://ssrn.com/abstract=3391331.

59  "Shocking Video: Law Professor Attacks Parental Rights," parentalrights.org, n.d., https://parentalrights.org/dwyer/.

60  "More Oversight Is Needed," Robert Reich, The New York Times, December 2, 2015, https://www.nytimes.com/roomfordebate/2011/01/04/do-home-schoolers-deserve-a-tax-break/more-oversight-is-needed.

61  Darren Jones, "Harvard Summit to Discuss Regulating Homeschooling," Home School Legal Defense Association, March 27, 2020, https://hslda.org/post/harvard-summit-to-discuss-regulating-homeschooling.

62  "Homeschooling Summit: Problems, Politics, and Prospects for Reform," June 18–19, 2020, https://cap.law.harvard.edu/wp-content/uploads/2020/01/Preliminary-Homeschooling-Conference-Agenda-For-Website-01.10.20.pdf.

- In 2007, UNESCO published a document titled "Demand-side financing in education."[63] The document outlines education financing restructuring to a voucher or education savings account (ESA), school-choice model that can allow governments more control over education curricula and aims to change behavior and increase equity. Other UNESCO documents, such as their Education 2030 Agenda and Sustainable Development Goal 4 titled "Global Citizenship Education," use progressive buzzwords to teach multiculturalism, gender identity, equality/equity, antiracism, diversity and inclusion, unconscious bias, and social justice.[64]

Of course, this is the language of their agendas and not what most people use, are aware of, or even understand. The trouble is that this is a tactic of these global institutions to confuse terminology and jumble up definitions to weaken people's objections to their objectives. Friendly-sounding terms obfuscate the fact that they mean the opposite. If an institution claims it's in favor of something, we can reasonably assume they desire the opposite or inverse. For example, when Harvard University sets lower admission score requirements for non-white students and demands higher test performance from white, Jewish, and Asian students, they claim it is absolutely not racial discrimination,[65] when it actually is.

There are hundreds of examples like this from academia's ivory towers, from the Ivy League to the United Nations and the activists and social engineers who support them. They not only lie to parents at every turn, but they also feel entitled to your children's attention so they can force them to memorize and adopt their lies as the truth. They will do this in any way they can, directly or indirectly. As mentioned, school choice vouchers, scholarships, and education spending accounts that are being pushed now

---

63 Harry Anthony Patrinos, "Demand-Side Financing in Education," UNESCO, 2007, https://unesdoc.unesco.org/in/documentViewer.xhtml?v=2.1.196&id=p::usmarcdef_0000181751&file=/in/rest/annotationSVC/DownloadWatermarkedAttachment/attach_import_0972b1a6-8397-4daf-a932-6ad0dcf78f43%3F_%3D181751eng.pdf&locale=en&multi=true&ark=/ark:/48223/pf0000181751/PDF/181751eng.pdf#%5B%7B%22num%22%3A105%2C%22gen%22%3A0%7D%2C%7B%22name%22%3A%22XYZ%22%7D%2Cnull%2Cnull%2C0%5D.

64 "Global Citizenship Education," UNESCO, n.d., https://en.unesco.org/themes/gced.

65 Lia Eustachewich, "Harvard's Gatekeeper Reveals SAT Cutoff Scores Based on Race," New York Post, October 17, 2018, https://nypost.com/2018/10/17/harvards-gatekeeper-reveals-sat-cutoff-scores-based-on-race/.

are an expansion of state control. At least their naked power grabs are out there for everyone to see. Even normies are beginning to wake up!

In more recent events, the closing of schools for the pandemic led to the greatest wake-up call of how bad government schools were. Parents saw their children de-stress and decompress from that oppressive system and realized that they could and should homeschool. Their relationships improved and led to a reconnection of the parent-child bonds. But ask yourselves, why did the Republicans dust off Newt Gingrich's old school voucher program from the 1990s during the pandemic? They called it "freedom" and even rebranded it as *school choice* even though it is more of an alternate accounting and funding plan. Was it a response to the grassroots homeschooling movement and seeing it as a threat to their power base? Was it to appease and placate parents who saw the real damage of government schools and wanting to homeschool? They just can't have people walk away and threaten the property tax plantation. Even the UNESCO documents describe vouchers (yes, School Choice is a UNESCO directive) as an alternate education financing methodology and not a "choice" movement. Always remember, government power has two boots: the left and the right. The fact is that vouchers are a back door to full regulation of homeschooling. When private schools take government money, they cede their hiring, enrollment, and curriculum to state mandates and control. It will be no different for homeschoolers—if families want the money, they have to jump through the hoops, and soon, there will be no independent homeschooling; families will be stuck with having to take the voucher.

*"Oh, but vouchers will bring in competition and get rid of bad teachers."* Really? Vouchers are another government program, and you still have a tax lien on your home. What competition? This is still a government monopoly but with an illusion of choice. Say you try to enroll your child at that private school with a voucher in hand, and they say, "Sorry, we have been hit with two hundred applications since the vouchers passed. We just don't have the room for the next eighteen months, and then there is a waiting list." What do you do now? How many people will file a class-action discrimination lawsuit against that private school, forcing it to close? So much for the competition. Don't be fooled; vouchers were offered to appease angry parents. Vouchers

are the chosen UNESCO financing model to regulate all education and ban independent homeschooling.

Stay informed about the laws, rules, and movements of the political landscape so you can be prepared to protect and defend your family. The laws passed may seem innocuous now, but that doesn't guarantee that these laws are not just the scaffolding for other agendas. Don't blindly trust the information politicians feed you—chances are they could be lying to you.

. . . .

Again, what you are doing by deciding to homeschool is that it is an act that has a far higher political return on investment than all other political activism combined – more than vouchers, and far more than beating your head on the podium at the school board meeting. Homeschooling is political power back into the hands of the Family – it provides a bulwark against the social contagions and degeneracy that your children would be exposed to and creates a better future for them. All it takes to harness that massive, multigenerational political power is to be *with* your children and raise/educate them in a way that is in their best interests.

# CHAPTER 14

# For Everyone

So as we have explained, kids don't need school. What was learned that they needed instead? And what, in short, is our radical new approach that prepares kids for the future and frees them to learn anything?

If we could condense this entire book into a single snippet, it would be this:

> *Instill and cultivate in your child their own agency and internal motivation. Use peaceful parenting and mentoring appropriate to your child's planes of development and sensibilities. Teach the knowledge and skills necessary for mastery using the three pillars of pedagogy. Cultivate in your children your family's values and virtues so they can become fully independent, fulfilled, and confident adults pursuing their own interests.*

Someone who hasn't finished this book won't fully grasp this statement. You do because you've read it. So if someone asks you what *Kids Don't Need School* is about, you can tell them, "You just have to read it. Trust me."

The book may be coming to a close, but our time together doesn't have to be. Because homeschooling is for everyone, we want to be helpful to as many people as we can and in as many ways as we can. There is more we at Homeschool Life can offer to help your homeschool run smoothly and deepen your parent-child bond.

# Homeschooling Beyond the Book

- **Homeschooling on a budget?** Subscribe to our free email newsletter where you'll get quick, easy homeschool tips and answers to frequently asked questions about raising self-learners. Simply visit www.homeschoollife.us to subscribe.

- **Want to connect with 400+ like-minded homeschool parents?** Join the Homeschool Life Community. Your premium membership includes exclusive access to helpful resources, useful workshops, and a private forum to ask any question and find the latest homeschooling news, law changes, and trends. Go to www.homeschoollife.us/become-a-member to join.

- **Need help now?** The fastest way to get immediate help with and actionable answers to your unique homeschooling challenge is to schedule a private consultation with a husband-and-wife team: Jonathan and Adriana. Book your session at www.homeschoollife.us/coaching.

*Thank you for reading this book.*

We'll be here if you would like any support or feedback. Now go and homeschool with confidence!


~Jonathan & Adriana Prescott

# Thank You

# Acknowledgements

This book would not have been possible without our friends and supporters. So many home educators who've come before us have inspired, encouraged, and taught us. Thank you for letting us stand on your shoulders or to stand beside you.

Specifically, we would like to express our gratitude for the works of Dr. Maria Montessori, Dr. Jean Piaget, Dr. Lawrence Kohlberg, Dr. Steven Reiss, Dr. Gabor Maté, John Taylor Gatto, John Holt, Elijah Stanfield of the Tuttle Twins, Stefan Molyneux, and Noah Revoy.

Thank you also to our senior writer and contributor at www.homeschoollife.us, Sysy Muñoz.

And a special thank you to Joshua Lisec, without whom this book would not exist.

# About the Authors

Jonathan and Adriana Prescott are trained engineers, serial entrepreneurs, and devoted parents. Their first book, Kids Don't Need School, shares their radical new approach to home education, prioritizing the parent-child bond, age-appropriate academic study, and pursuit of mastery over grades. Their private online homeschoolers community, Homeschool Life, puts their principles into practice, resulting in self-taught children who are ten to fifteen years ahead of their traditionally schooled peers.

Jonathan and Adriana have been married for two decades, have one living child whom they've homeschooled her entire life, and call Kennewick, Washington home. Get homeschool support from experienced, like-minded educators at www.homeschoollife.us.

# Appendix: List of Illustrations and Charts

## Figure 1: The Three Pillars of Pedagogy

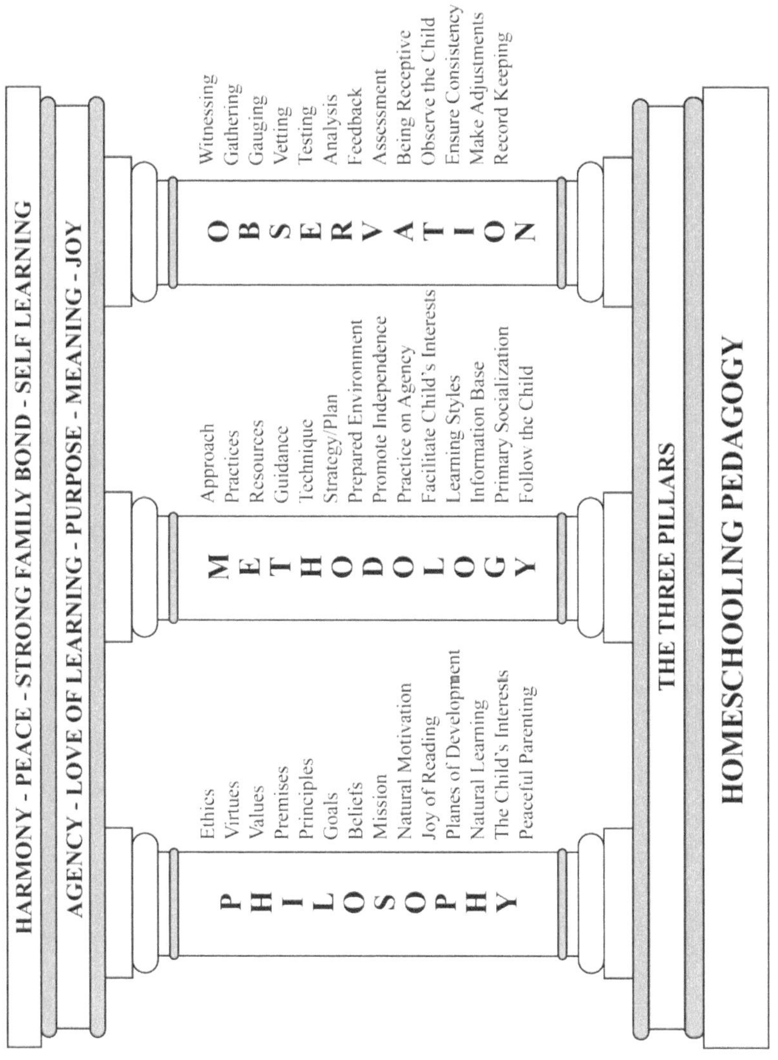

# Figure 2: The Four Planes of Development

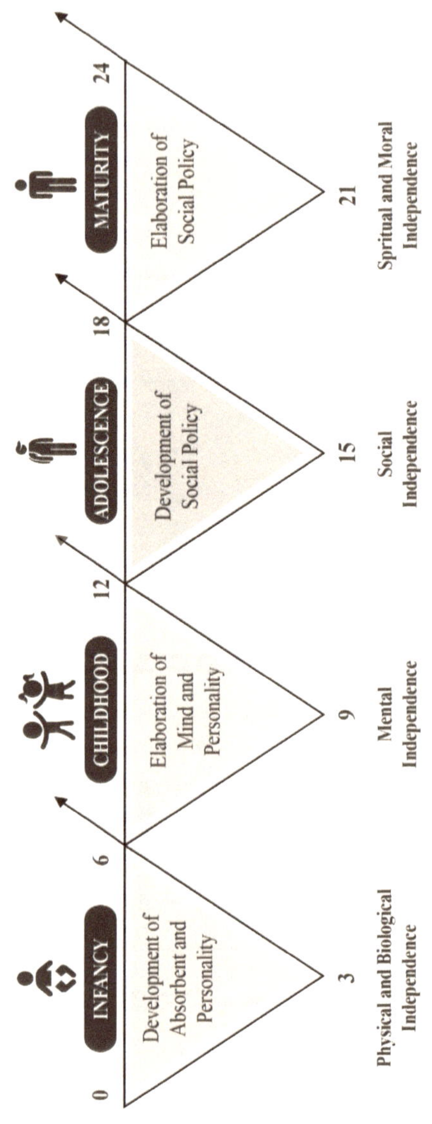

# Figure 3: Sustained Attention by Grade

## SUSTAINED ATTENTION BY GRADE

| Grade Level | Minimum | Maximum | Recommended Length Sustained Attention |
| --- | --- | --- | --- |
| PreK | 20 minutes/day | 60 minutes/day | 3-5 minutes |
| K | 30 minutes/day | 90 minutes/day | 3-5 minutes |
| 1-2 | 45 minutes/day | 90 minutes/day | 5-10 minutes |
| 3-5 | 60 minutes/day | 120 minutes/day | 10-15 minutes |
| 6-8 | Class: 15 minutes/day<br>Total: 90 minutes/day | Class: 30 minutes/day<br>Class: 180 minutes/day | 1 subject area or class |
| 9-12 | Class: 20 minutes/day<br>Total: 120 minutes/day | Class: 45 minutes/day<br>Class: 270 minutes/day | 1 subject area or class |